Starting
SPSS/PC+

– a beginner's guide to data analysis

Jeremy J. Foster

SIGMA PRESS – *Wilmslow, United Kingdom*

First published in 1992 by

Sigma Press, 1 South Oak Lane, Wilmslow, Cheshire SK9 6AR, England.

British Library Cataloguing in Publication Data

A CIP catalogue record for this book is available from the British Library.

ISBN: 1-85058-263-7

Typesetting and design by

Sigma Hi-Tech Services Ltd

Printed in Malta by
Interprint Ltd.

Distributed by

John Wiley & Sons Ltd., Baffins Lane, Chichester, West Sussex, England.

Preface

This book is designed to teach beginners how to operate SPSS/PC+. Let's suppose you have some data and some questions such as *"How do I get a frequency table, an average or a histogram?"* The book gives you the answers, explaining the commands you need, and showing you the output the commands provide. It is not a text in statistical analysis; I have assumed that the person who comes to SPSS/PC+ is likely to know, at least in general terms, what statistical analysis they want to do. What they do not know is how to get SPSS/PC+ to do it for them! Appendix B provides a brief recapitulation on statistical analysis for readers who feel a bit 'rusty'.

The book is intended for the individual student or researcher who has access to a PC with SPSS/PC+ installed; moving between the computer and the written explanation is the only way to develop skill at using the program. It uses a set of hypothetical data as the basis for the various analyses described. Do please carry out the various examples and exercises: it is only by having hands-on practice that you will develop an understanding of the way SPSS/PC+ works, and become its master.

Finally, a word of hope: SPSS/PC+ is very efficient, but it is complicated. Do not become discouraged if at first you find it confusing: we all do! Once you have mastered the general principles, you will soon find that it is comparatively straightforward to obtain the results you want. And remember that when you are able to drive SPSS/PC+, you have enormous power at your disposal.

Jeremy Foster

Acknowledgements

Thanks are extended to SPSS UK Ltd for permission to use copies of SPSS/PC+ screens.

SPSS is a registered trademark and the other product names are trademarks of SPSS Inc.

For information about SPSS contact:

SPSS UK Ltd., SPSS House, 5, London Street, Chertsey, Surrey KT 16 8AP.

Tel: 0932 566262; Fax: 0932 567020

CONTENTS

1

The Aims of this Book

1.1 Introduction

The fact that you are reading this book means you are thinking of using SPSS/PC+. You are probably already aware that SPSS/PC+ is a set of programs that allows you rapidly to analyse data, huge amounts of data, and that using SPSS/PC+ you can carry out in a few moments statistical analysis that would be impractical without the aid of a computer. You may already have come across the manuals to SPSS/PC+ and have probably found them extremely daunting! The manuals are not really intended as a teaching medium; they are designed to help those who already know what they are doing with SPSS/PC+. This book is intended to show you how to operate SPSS/PC+ so that you can analyse data which you want analysed.

This is not a book on statistics, because you are likely to know the analyses you want, if not how to obtain them. There is only a very brief explanation of the various statistical procedures, but you will find a short description of the output that SPSS/PC+ provides, as users do not always find the printed output completely clear, and a summary of the principles of statistical analysis is given in Appendix B.

This book covers most of the facilities offered by the Base module of version 3 of SPSS/PC+Computer, the version in most common use in 1991. (How version 4.0 differs from version 3 is explained below in 1.2.) I have structured the text by considering the questions that the user asks, moving from the simpler to the more complex procedures. Manuals are often written the other way round; they explain the various commands one after the other, giving you the answer before you understand the question. While this means the manual describes everything the program will do, it also means that users cannot readily find the answers they are seeking.

I have tried to anticipate the problems you are most likely to come across, and to explain how to deal with them. Some of the simpler problems that confuse beginners are listed in Chapter 27, and others are described at appropriate points in the text.

SPSS/PC+ offers you a very wide range of options when analysing your data. I have not attempted to cover everything you can do with it; the most important thing is for the beginner to gain familiarity and understanding with the way the program operates, and this can best be done by using the most frequently used procedures. Once you are confident with them, you will be able to understand the manuals, and be able to see how the more advanced procedures which they describe can be applied to your needs.

If you are unfamiliar with PCs, a simple description is given in Chapter 2. This information may be helpful if you are uncertain about such things as the difference between a floppy disk and a hard disk, or what the less familiar keys on the keyboard do.

If you are unfamiliar with DOS, and the difference between DOS and programs such as SPSS/PC+, do read Chapter 3. I have found, when teaching SPSS/PC+, that many beginners get confused and try to run DOS commands from SPSS/PC+ or vice versa. So if you are unclear about the idea of directory structures, renaming and copying files or what a batch file is, take the time to go through Chapter 3. Resist the temptation to get stuck straight into the chapter on Starting Out: you do need to understand the elementary features of DOS before you launch yourself into SPSS/PC+.

1.2 Note on version 4.0 of SPSS/PC+

This book was written with and for SPSS/PC+ Version 3.1, which has been superseded (1991) by version 4.0. Most readers will probably have version 3, but those with version 4.0 will find that their version operates in the same manner as that described here.

The main change with version 4.0 is that there is now a separate Statistics option in addition to the Advanced Statistics option.

The version 4.0 Base system includes the following procedures which are described in this book: AUTORECODE, COMPUTE, CROSSTABS, DESCRIPTIVES, EXA-MINE, FREQUENCIES, JOIN, LIST, MEANS, N, PLOT, PLOT/FORMAT REGRESSION, PROCESS IF, RANK, RECODE, REPORT, SAVE, SELECT IF, SORT, YRMODA. It also contains some procedures which are not considered here, as they are unlikely to be needed by a beginner: AGGREGATE, FLIP, WRITE, EXPORT.

Most important, a number of the useful statistical procedures previously included in the base system are not included in that for version 4.0, having been made part of the Statistics option. These are: ANOVA, CORRELATION, NPAR (and the non-parametric tests), ONEWAY, REGRESSION, T-TEST. The operation of these procedures is included in this book, since they feature in version 3.0 and 3.1, and are likely to be needed by many users.

1.3 Conventions used in the printing of this book

As you work through the exercises and examples, you have to key in material from the keyboard, and press specified keys to achieve particular results. When you have to type in words and numbers, they are printed like this:

`type a:exdat (R)`

This means you should type in from the keyboard exactly what is shown in this format, including, in this example, the word `type`. Pressing the Return key (also known as the Enter key) is shown as `(R)`.

You will need to make regular use of the Function keys, marked F1 to F10 on your keyboard. These are named as F1, F2 and so on: remember this does not mean you press the letter F and then a number, but the appropriate Function key.

Your keyboard has a set of keys for controlling the movement of the cursor on the screen. They are labelled on the keyboard with arrows pointing up, down, left and right and are named in the text as up-arrow, down-arrow, left-arrow and right-arrow. The keys labelled PgUp, PgDn, Home, End, Ins are referred to by their names, as are the Esc (Escape), Alt and Ctrl keys.

Your keyboard contains two or three keys marked Del. The one needed most of the time is the -Del key, which will be referred to as the Del key. When you need the Del key included in the number pad to the right of the keyboard, this will be referred to as the number/Del key.

There will be many occasions when you need to press two keys together, for example the Alt and E keys. To do this, you press down the Alt key and while it is depressed tap the E key, then release the Alt key. This is shown in the text as Alt E, but remember it does not mean that you press the Alt key followed by the E key: the Alt key must be held down when you press the E key.

2

Simple Introduction to the PC

2.1 Hardware

You are probably familiar with the basic physical components of the PC: a screen (VDU) and a keyboard which are attached to the unit housing the various electronic components that form the 'works' of the machine and which has a floppy disk drive incorporated in it. In addition there may be a mouse, and to use SPSS/PC+ you really need a printer. The program runs without one, but you will want to obtain a printed copy of the output so you can study it at leisure.

PC is rather a simplification, since there are various kinds. There are, of course, many different makes of PC, but the name on the outside of the box is not particularly important: it is what is inside the box, the type of chip that forms the central processor, that distinguishes one kind from another. The original PCs, the PC XT, has an 8088 processor, whereas the more modern one, the PC AT has an 80286, 80386 or 80486 processor.

Screens vary in terms of their physical size, and whether they are monochrome or colour. (Colour displays vary in terms of their sophistication, and you will come across terms such as EGA and VGA which describe different types, but you can happily remain ignorant of such matters.) The physical size of the screen is unimportant, as there will be 80 columns available in one line of characters whatever the physical dimensions of the screen. If you are using SPSS/PC+ with a colour display, you will find that the screen is divided into differently coloured sections; if yours is a monochrome display, the differences will be in whether the sections are light on dark or dark on light.

PCs vary in terms of the number and size of disk drives they have. The simpler machines have just one floppy disk drive (5.25'' or 3.5''). The next grade up has two floppy drives, and the top category has one floppy drive and a hard disk incorporated inside the unit. You can only use SPSS/PC+ on a PC that has a hard disk, which can store much more information than a floppy. Most 5 1/4 inch disks contain just over 360k, most 3 1/2 inch disks just over 720k; k here refers to thousands of bytes of information, so 360k means 360,000 bytes.

High density disks, which require high density drives to use their full potential, contain 1.2 Mb and 1.44 Mb respectively. Mb denotes a megabyte, or million bytes of information, so 1.2 Mb is almost four times as much as 360k. You can use low density disks on a high density drive, but it is not possible to use high density disks on a low density drive. A hard disk will contain 20, 30, 40 or even more Mb and is needed because SPSS/PC+ itself takes up so much memory.

This book assumes you are sitting in front of a PC that has SPSS/PC+ installed on it, which means it has a hard disk and at least one floppy disk drive. (Whether it uses 5 1/4 or 3 1/2 inch disks does not matter, so long as you have a disk of the correct size!)

2.2 The keyboard

There are different styles of keyboard, with the various sets of keys in different positions. Make sure you can identify the main letter and number keys which are in the traditional QWERTY layout, and the shift key which gives you upper case letters and the symbols written on the number keys above the numbers themselves.

In addition to these, your keyboard will have a set of Function keys, labelled F1 to F10, and another set of keys on the right of the keyboard which control the movement of the cursor on the screen. They have arrows and numbers on them. There is another key labelled NumLock. With NumLock on, these 'arrow keys' have the effect of entering numbers, but we shall be using the cursor movement facilities, so make sure the NumLock key is in the off position. (There will be an indicator light on the keyboard which is on when NumLock is on. Make sure it is off; if it is on, press the NumLock key and it will go out.)

There are two or three Del (Delete) keys. One is on the top right of the main section of the keyboard and may be marked -Del or have a left-pointing arrow. There is another in the number keypad on the right of the keyboard which can also function as a decimal point key. For most purposes use the -Del key, which deletes the character to the left of the position where the cursor is placed. The number keypad Del, which will be referred to as number/Del, deletes the character at the point the cursor is placed when the key is pressed; characters to the right of the cursor position move left to fill the gap.

The Alt and Ctrl keys are rather like shift keys in that they modify the meaning of pressing an ordinary key if that key is pressed while Alt or Ctrl is depressed. Esc (for

Escape) is used to cancel certain operations. Ins (which stands for Insert) switches you from Insert mode to Overtype mode, and is explained in Section 8.1.

The Return or Enter key has different effects, depending upon the task you are doing at the keyboard. When you are typing in, it causes the cursor to finish a line and move to the beginning of the next one. It is also used to instruct the computer to carry out the command and within SPSS/PC+ to select items from menus. **In this book, pressing the Return key is shown by (R).**

2.3 Floppy disks

Once installed, the various programs that make up SPSS/PC+ are stored on the hard disk in a directory labelled SPSS. It is perfectly feasible to store the data you want analysed and the results of the analysis on the hard disk, but hard disks can 'crash' (i.e. fail) so whatever is stored on them is lost. Furthermore, if you store your files on the hard disk they are not portable. But when stored on a floppy, they can be taken to any PC that has SPSS/PC+ installed on it, and used on that machine. So you are not tied to one PC, and can make copies of your data and command files so that you have a back up copy in case disaster strikes and your floppy gets damaged.

2.4 Formatting a floppy disk

When you buy a new disk, it cannot be used until it has been formatted. This divides it into sections and creates a map telling the computer what is in the various sections and how to get to them. All this is electronic and invisible, of course. A disk needs to be formatted just once, so only if you have acquired a new disk do you need to do the following before using it. If the PC has one floppy disk drive, it is drive A. (On a PC with two drives, the upper or left one is drive A and the other is drive B. If you put the disk into drive B, then type: B: rather than A: in the following instructions).

❏ Do not put the disk into the drive

❏ Make sure the machine is on and showing the DOS prompt: *C:\>*

❏ Put the disk into the drive and close the door.

❏ Type: format a: (R). It is vital to have a space between t and a, but no space between a and :

❏ If you press *;* rather than : do not press (R), but use the -Del key to remove the *;* and then type in :

If you type in the wrong instruction, the computer will probably come back to you telling you it could not read drive A and ask you to *Abort, Retry, Ignore?* If this happens, press A (for Abort) and when the prompt *C:\>* re-appears, try again after making sure the disk is in the correct drive and the door is closed. If all else fails, take the disk out, switch the computer off and then start again.

The formatting process will take place (it takes a minute or so). When it is finished the screen will show how many bytes are available on the disk and ask: *Format another? (y/n)*

Type in n (R) and the screen will return to the C:\> prompt.

2.5 Warning for beginners: switch on without a disk

When switching the computer on, make sure the floppy disk is NOT in the disk drive. If you do switch on with a disk in the drive, the computer will try to read DOS programs from it, and unless it is a special type of disk it will not contain them; the computer will then tell you the drive contains the wrong type of disk (not a system disk). If this happens, take the disk out of the drive, switch the computer off, count to 10 and switch on again. When the prompt C:\> appears, put the disk into the drive.

3

Simple Introduction to DOS

3.1 What is DOS?

When the computer is turned on, it automatically loads a disk operating system, DOS, which is a set of programs that controls the way the computer operates. (Different PCs have different versions of DOS, but they are similar in the way the user interacts with them.)

It is important for the beginner to appreciate the difference between DOS and the SPSS/PC+ programs, because you can do things in DOS that you cannot do in SPSS/PC+, and vice versa.

You know that you are at the DOS level when you first switch the machine on, because the screen will display the prompt C:\>. (It is quite easy to alter this, so that the prompt contains some message. Your screen may show additional information such as the date.) This means the system is connected to drive C (the hard disk inside the computer box), and is ready to receive orders.

3.2 Simple DOS commands

The most simple DOS commands are explained in the sections below. When you type in a DOS command, the case of the letters is unimportant, so DIR and dir have the same effect. But the spaces between components of the commands are crucial, as they distinguish one part of the command from another. So, for example, when using the rename command, the space between fn1 and fn2 in the command:

```
rename a:fn1 fn2
```

is a necessity. If you typed in:

`a:fn1fn2`

you would get a message indicating that DOS cannot understand the instruction, so do ensure you type in the commands with the spaces.

3.3 Seeing a list of the files on your disk: DIR

The various programs and files on the computer are stored on the hard disk, and the first thing you can do is see a list of the programs on the hard disk, by typing in:

`dir (R)`

This tells DOS to put on the screen a list of the programs on the disk drive to which the system is connected. So when the machine has just been switched on, `dir (R)` yields a list of the programs on the hard disk (drive C). The list may be longer than the number of lines on the screen, and it will scroll off the top. The machine will show the list one screenful at a time if you use the command:

`dir/p (R)`

The listing of the files will pause when the screen is full; press any key to continue the listing. It is complete when the screen indicates the number of bytes available on the disk.

The list of programs is known as a directory; think of it as a catalogue, showing the contents of a library of programs. Different kinds of items are listed, each with a name and many also have a suffix (known as a filename extension) listed in a second column on the screen. Examples of the extension are BAT, EXE and COM.

One program is shown as: AUTOEXEC BAT. The true name of this program is AUTOEXEC.BAT i.e. it is the name from the first column of the directory listing followed by a full stop and then the extension. The extension indicates what kind of program or file it is. For example, a file with the extension .BAT is a Batch File which contains a number of commands for the computer.

Some kinds of file can be listed on the screen as recognisable words, but others (such as .EXE files) are written in a special code and any attempt to list them on the screen will give sets of meaningless symbols. Do not worry if this happens: it does no harm to the computer or the program file.

3.4 The directory structure

The directory shown after first switching on and then typing in `dir (R)` is known as the root directory. Some of the entries in the list have the extension <DIR>, like this:

```
SPSS <DIR>
```

This extension means that there is a subdirectory within the main directory. A subdirectory contains its own set of programs, and to see what they are it is necessary to move into that subdirectory.

There may be a large number of subdirectories, and a subdirectory can contain further subdirectories, so the structure resembles a tree with many branches and sub-branches as illustrated in Figure 3.1. To keep the filing system in reasonable order, programs or files associated with a particular application are usually stored in their own subdirectory. For example, all the files concerned with a word processor will be stored in one subdirectory, all the files concerned with SPSS/PC+ in another, and so on.

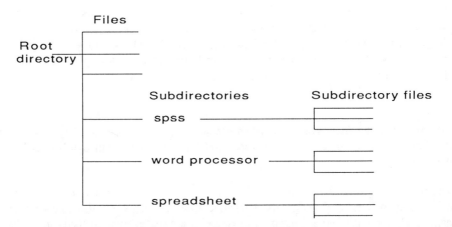

Figure 3.1: Diagram of the file structure of DOS

3.5 Changing directories

To change from the root directory to the subsidiary one called SPSS, type:

```
cd SPSS (R)
```

which means *Change to the directory labelled SPSS*. The screen prompt will change to C:\SPSS>, indicating that the system is now in the subdirectory labelled SPSS. Note that the cd command does NOT tell the computer to run the programs contained in the subdirectory; it simply tells it to move to the subdirectory.

To find out what is in that subdirectory, type in:

```
dir (R)
```

and the contents of the subdirectory are shown on the screen.

To move back to the root directory, enter:

`cd\ (R)`

The prompt will go back to C:\>. The back-slash character, \, indicates the system is in the root directory.

3.6 Creating a new subdirectory

To create a subdirectory called PROJECT on the hard disk, make sure you are in the root directory of the hard disk and type:

`md PROJECT (R)`

A directory listing will then include PROJECT <DIR>, showing that there is now a subdirectory with that name.

3.7 Changing drives

When first switched on, the computer addresses the hard disk, drive C. The floppy disk drive is drive A (or A and B if there are two). To have the machine communicate automatically with the floppy disk drive, follow these steps:

❑ Put a formatted disk into the drive. Type: A: (R) and the prompt will become A:\>

❑ You can then obtain a directory listing of what is on the floppy disk by keying in: dir (R)

❑ To return to communicating with the hard disk, type: C: (R) and the prompt will become C:\>.

3.8 Telling the system where a file is

Most DOS instructions tell the computer to carry out some operation on a named file or program. For example, the command:

`type autoexec.bat (R)`

instructs the system to list to the screen the file called autoexec.bat. When giving an instruction like this, you must remember which drive the system is addressing, and which contains the file or program it is to operate upon. The system will automatically look for a file or program in the drive and directory that it is currently connected to.

For example, if the system is addressing drive C and is in the root directory (the prompt is C:\>), you can list a file in the root directory (such as autoexec.bat) by simply typing:

`type autoexec.bat (R)`

When the file wanted is not in the current drive and directory, you must specify the drive and/or directory within the DOS instruction. If the system is addressing drive C and you want to list on the screen a file (suppose it is called ex.lis) that is on the floppy disk (drive A), you must tell DOS that the file wanted is on a different drive by preceding the name of the file with the drive name. So you would need to type in:

`type a:ex.lis (R)`

If the system is addressing drive A already, it shows the prompt A:\>. To list a file (ex.lis, for example) that is on the floppy disk (drive A), you don't have to specify the drive, and can just use the command:

`type ex.lis (R)`

Here is another example. In the subdirectory SPSS on the hard disk there is a file called SPSS.LIS. How can you have it listed on the screen? The answer depends on where you are in the system. If you are connected to the C drive and are in the SPSS subdirectory, the screen prompt will be C:\SPSS>. You can then just type in:

`type spss.LIS (R)`

If you are in the root directory of the hard disk, the prompt shows C:\> and you have to tell the computer that the file you want is in a subdirectory by preceding the filename with the subdirectory name like this:

`type \spss\spss.lis (R)`

The \ characters are essential, as they tell DOS that in this line `spss` is the name of a subdirectory, and `spss.lis` is the name of a file.

If you are connected to drive A, and the screen prompt is A:\>, you have to indicate that the file you want is on a different drive and specify its directory by typing in:

`type c:\spss\spss.lis (R)`

If you ask the computer to apply a command to a file and receive the message *File not found*, this is often because the file is not in the drive or directory that the system is currently addressing. Another frequent error which produces the same message is to type in a filename that the system does not recognise, because the spelling is not exactly the same as the name under which the file is stored. If you receive the *File not found* message, repeat the command, making sure that, if necessary, you specify the drive and/or directory of the file in the DOS instruction, and are using the correct filename.

3.9 Listing a file on the screen: TYPE

The following sections assume you have read Section 3.8.

To list a file on the screen use the DOS command:

```
type fn (R)
```

but use the name of the file in place of `fn`. So to see the contents of the AUTOEXEC.BAT file, enter:

```
type AUTOEXEC.BAT (R)
```

Lengthy files will scroll off the screen. To pause the listing, use CTRL S. Use this combination again to restart the listing.

3.10 Printing a file: TYPE...>PRN

To print a file, make sure the printer is switched on, loaded with paper and is on line. This means it has a channel of communication with the computer. There will be a button on your printer marked *On Line*, and an indicator light associated with it. This light must be on; if it is out, press the On Line button on the printer and check the indicator light is illuminated. Then use this command, but type in the name of the file instead of `fn`:

```
type fn >PRN (R)
```

3.11 Changing the name of a file

Changing the name of a file does just that: it simply alters the title, but not the contents. From drive C, to change the name of a file stored on the floppy disk (drive A) from fn1 to fn2, type:

```
rename a:fn1 fn2 (R)
```

If the system is addressing drive A, so the prompt is A:\>, just type:

```
rename fn1 fn2 (R)
```

The space between `fn1` and `fn2` is crucial. The file that was called fn1 will now be called fn2.

3.12 Copying a file

From the root directory of drive C, to copy a file called fn1, which is in a subdirectory called subdir, to the floppy disk (drive A), type:

`copy C:\subdir\fn1 A:(R)`

Remember to replace `subdir` with the name of the subdirectory in which the file is stored, and `fn1` with the real name of the file to be copied. It is essential to include the space between the last character of the filename and the letter indicating the destination drive. As an example, the following command copies the file spss.lis from the subdirectory spss to the floppy disk:

`copy \spss\spss.lis a: (R)`

If you were in the spss subdirectory on drive C, the copy could be achieved with the instruction:

`copy spss.lis a: (R)`

To copy a file named fn from the floppy disk into the subdirectory called subdir on the hard disk, get into the root directory of drive C and type:

`copy a:fn c:\subdir (R)`

Put the name of the subdirectory into which the file is to be copied in place of the word `subdir` in this instruction. For example, to copy a file called mydat from the floppy disk (drive A) into a directory on the hard disk called PROJECT, type:

`copy A:mydat C:\PROJECT (R)`

The directory called PROJECT must exist on the hard disk before this command is used. Section 3.6 explains how to create a subdirectory.

What is SPSS/PC+?

4.1 Overview of the Structure of SPSS/PC+

SPSS/PC+ is a suite of computer programs, developed over many years. The original SPSS and SPSSx were only available on main-frame computers. The PC version is now becoming one of the most widely-used programs of its type in the world. The main development over the main-frame versions was SPSS/PC+ V2.0, which incorporated a menu-driven front end. Further modifications are appearing regularly, with version 4 being the current one, but the general structure of the program is likely to remain stable. A Macintosh SPSS/PC+ is now available, using the familiar Mac front end.

All users will have the Base system of SPSS/PC+. In addition, you can purchase extra modules such as Data Entry and the Tables module. These are not considered in this book, which uses only the Base system. Even this consists of a large set of programs, as you will see if you do a directory listing when you are at the DOS level and in the SPSS directory on your hard disk. (The directory listing is not particularly informative; SPSS/PC+ includes a system manager which allows you to obtain a more helpful indication of what your system contains. A simple introduction to the system manager is given in Chapter 26).

As a beginner, you do not need to know much about the actual SPSS/PC+ programs; the important thing is learning to drive rather than learning how the car works! But SPSS/PC+ is rather complicated, and it is important to understand the general characteristics of the structure of the program and the files it uses and creates.

Figure 4.1 indicates the way in which the files are organised. (In this book it is assumed the data and command files are stored on a floppy disk, and that one of the output files, the .LIS file is also sent to the floppy disk.) Essentially, SPSS/PC+ sits on the hard disk, usually in a directory called SPSS. In order to use SPSS/PC+ you

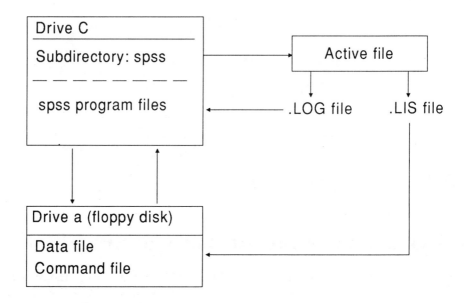

Figure 4.1: Diagram of the structure of SPSS/PC+ files

must provide it with data to be analysed, and this is stored in a data file. When you want the data to be analysed, you have to tell SPSS/PC+ how the data in the data file is organised and what analysis you want done on it. This set of data descriptions and instructions is included in a command file. You have to create the data and command files.

When SPSS/PC+ runs, it reads the commands from the command file and makes a copy of the data from the data file in another file known as the Active File. It then follows the commands from the command file, using the copy of the data in the Active File. The Active File is lost when you leave SPSS/PC+.

When it is running, SPSS/PC+ creates two output files. One is the file that holds the results of the analysis it has performed; unless you tell it otherwise, this results file is called SPSS.LIS. The other output file is named SPSS.LOG, and records a list of the commands which SPSS/PC+ is carrying out.

There is one important fact to understand about the .LIS and .LOG files. When you first enter SPSS/PC+, the SPSS.LIS and SPSS.LOG files in the subdirectory SPSS on drive C are wiped clean, ready for the results of a new run of the program. So you need to make sure you have saved the results of any previous run of the program in a file that will not be wiped. How this is done is explained as you work through this book (e.g. Chapter 9).

Remember that SPSS/PC+ is distinct from DOS. The various DOS commands described in Chapter 3 cannot be entered directly from SPSS/PC+. So you cannot be in SPSS/PC, type in a DOS command such as:

```
type a:ex1.lis>prn (R)
```

and expect it to work: it won't! There are ways of entering DOS commands into a set of SPSS/PC+ commands, but they do require a special form, as is described in Chapter 9. For the moment, try to remember that DOS and SPSS/PC+ are different!

5

Starting Out with SPSS/PC+

5.1 What you need to run SPSS/PC+

Assuming SPSS/PC+ is installed on your hard disk, there are six things you need in order to use it:

❏ To know how to get to the SPSS/PC+ programs

❏ A file of data to be analysed, which you will write

❏ A set of commands telling SPSS/PC+ how the data is laid out and precisely what analysis you want it to do. These are included in the Command File, which you write

❏ To know how to get SPSS/PC+ to apply the command file to the data file; in other words, how to run SPSS/PC+

❏ To know how to examine the contents of the output (.LIS) file

❏ To know how to get the .LIS file stored on the floppy disk, and in such a way that it will not be overwritten the next time SPSS/PC+ runs.

These requirements are covered in the following chapters. To begin, how do you get into SPSS/PC+ (and how do you get out of it)?

5.2 Getting to SPSS/PC+

If SPSS/PC+ has been installed on your PC in the usual way, it will be stored on your hard disk in a directory entitled SPSS. To get into the program:

❏ Switch on

❏ At the C:\> prompt, type: cd SPSS (R)

❏ The screen prompt will become C:\SPSS>

❏ Type: SPSSPC (R)

The program will then load; you will first of all see the title screen, and after a few moments the main entry screen, shown in Figure 5.1 will appear. Before you do anything else it is worth taking a few moments just to look at the screen, as it has a number of components.

5.3 The entry screen

The screen is divided into four sections. In the upper left there is a section headed MAIN MENU, with one entry (orientation) highlighted in light on dark; other entries are dark on light. When SPSS/PC+ starts, it automatically goes into menu mode, and you can move this highlighting cursor up and down the menu using the arrow keys on the keyboard. (If your version of the program has been modified so that the screen you are now looking at does not contain the Main menu, press Alt M. The screen will then look like Figure 5.1)

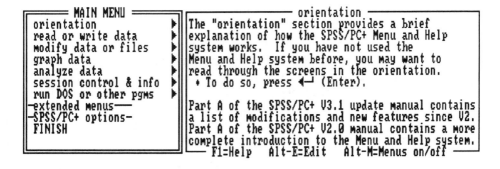

Figure 5.1: The initial SPSS/PC+ screen

In the upper right part of the screen there is a window that shows information about whatever is highlighted in the menu. As the cursor in the menu is moved using the arrow keys, the information in the information window changes. As you use SPSS/PC+, do keep referring to the information window: it is helpful! If necessary, scroll the information window with Alt down-arrow.

The lower half of the screen is the scratchpad, which is where you write in data or commands when you are creating files. When you first enter SPSS/PC+, the scratchpad is empty.

The last section of the screen is the bottom two lines. As you use the system, various messages and minimenus will appear on the bottom line. At present it simply reads *scratchpad*, the name of the file in the lower part of the screen.

The line above the bottom line contains information. There is a small window which says *Ins*; this means you are in Insert mode. If you press the Ins key on your keyboard, this message will disappear (you will be in Overtype mode). Get back to Insert mode by pressing the Ins key again. There is also a counter on the far right which tells you the column in which the cursor in the scratchpad is placed; at the moment it says *01* because the cursor is in column 1, the top left of the lower half of the screen.

5.4 Menu mode and edit mode

SPSS/PC+ can be run in different modes. In menu mode, when you move the cursor with the up-arrow and down-arrow keys (or the mouse), the cursor in the menu moves up and down, and you can select items from the menu and paste them into the scratchpad. (When you are familiar with using the package you may find the menu system rather laborious and easier to do without. But for beginners it is very helpful and we shall be using it throughout this book.) In menu mode you can NOT type from the keyboard directly into the scratchpad. If you want to do that, you must be in edit mode. Similarly, when you are in edit mode you can type directly into the scratchpad, but cannot select items from the menu in the upper left quadrant.

There is a range of editing facilities in the scratchpad that allows you to correct or alter the text or data you type in. You move the typing cursor around using the arrow keys, and type in new material which will be inserted at the point where the cursor was placed. The fact that you are in Insert mode is shown by *Ins* being displayed at the bottom of the screen. To switch to Overtype mode, where what you type will overwrite the existing characters, press the Ins key on the keyboard; the *Ins* message on the screen will disappear.

5.5 Switching between menu and edit modes

At various times you are likely to try actions when you are in the wrong mode. If you try to select a menu item when you are in edit mode, the cursor will not move around the menu as you expect; pressing the arrow keys will move the scratchpad cursor, not the menu cursor. On the other hand, if you try to type in when you are in menu mode, you will get a warning beep and the message *Not found,* followed by a window showing the characters you typed, will appear on the bottom line. Remove this window by pressing the Escape key. On other occasions you will try to do something but the system will tell you that it is not possible to do it when you are in menu mode. (This occurs with some of the Function keys, which are explained a little later on).

Whenever you are in the wrong mode, you need to switch to the other mode, using Alt E, before trying the instruction again. When switching from menu mode to edit mode, the message *Edit mode- press Esc to resume menu mode* will appear on the left of the bottom line of the screen, and the cursor in the scratchpad will become a flashing underline character. When switching from edit to menu mode, the message *Loading menu* will appear briefly at the bottom left of the screen, and the cursor will become a flashing square.

5.6 Using the menus

In menu mode, move up and down the menu using the arrow keys on the keyboard. Words in capitals in the menu are SPSS/PC+ commands. You select these and add them to the file being built up in the scratchpad by moving the cursor until the command is highlighted and then pressing (R).

If a menu entry has an arrowhead to its right, there is a subsidiary menu; to reach it, put the menu cursor over that item and press the right-arrow key on the keyboard. The subsidiary menu will then appear in the menu quadrant, and relevant information will appear in the information window. For example, the starting position is shown in Figure 5.1. If you move the cursor down to the entry *read or write data* and then press the right arrow key you will find the screen changes. The menu now has a different title (*read or write data*, in this example) and a fresh set of entries: *DE, GET* and so on.

The menu system goes to six levels, and it is easy to get lost! To get back up a level in the menus, press the left-arrow key on the keyboard. To jump straight back to the top level Main Menu press Alt Esc.

Although the menu system is intended to be helpful (and is, once you become familiar with it!), the titles of the menus are not always self-explanatory; commands can be difficult to find. Chapter 28 provides a summary of the menu structure, showing where the main commands are.

The menu system which operates when you first enter SPSS/PC+ is known as the standard menus. You can ask for an even larger menu system by pressing Alt X, which invokes the Extended Menus. A window in the bottom right of the screen will indicate if you are using extended menus. In this book, we shall use the Standard Menus, but you can explore the Extended Menus at any time by pressing Alt X.

5.7 Removing and restoring the menus

To remove the menu, press Alt M. The menu and information windows will disappear, you will be put into edit mode, and the top half of the screen will show the output .LIS file. (If you remove the menus before you have run an SPSS/PC+ application, the top half of the screen will be blank.)

To restore the menus, press Alt M again. You will automatically be put into menu mode.

5.8 What the Function keys do

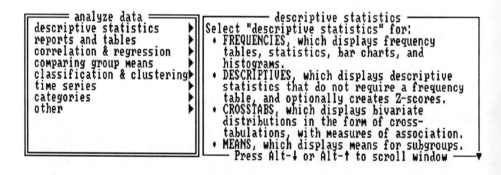

Figure 5.2: The screen when F9 has been pressed

Note: The *analyze data* entry from the main menu has been selected and the right arrow key pressed to reveal the submenu shown in the menu section of the screen.

Various facilities are available if you press the Function keys (F1 - F10), each of which produces a minimenu along the bottom line of the screen. When you press F9, for example, this minimenu appears, see Figure 5.2.

file: write Whole file   Delete

To select any of the options available, move the cursor along the line with the arrow keys, and when the cursor is over the desired choice press (R). Alternatively, each option has one capital letter in its title, which you can use to select that entry.

The uses of the Function keys are shown in Fig 5.3 (by function) and Fig 5.4 (by key). A screen display showing the uses of the Function keys is obtained by pressing F1 and selecting *Review help*. To remove the display, press Esc.

Change size of window	F2
Change strings in a file	F5
Delete a block of lines	F8
Delete a file from disk	F9
Delete a single line from a file	F4
Find strings in a file	F5
Glossary	F1
Go to particular page in a file	F6
Insert a single line in a file	F4
List of files	F1
List of variables in the Active File	F1
Mark columns of figures in a file	F7
Mark a block of lines in a file	F7
Move a block of lines in a file	F8
Move a single line in a file	F4
On-screen help	F1
Retrieve a file from floppy disk	F3
Round numbers off	F8
Run SPSS/PC+	F10
Save a file	F9
Switch windows	F2
System prompt	F10

Figure 5.3: Main uses of the Function keys by function

F1   For obtaining Help information, a list of files on your floppy
            disk, using the Glossary.
            Submenu:
            info: Review help Var list File list Glossary menu Hlp off

F2   For switching between windows and changing window size.
            Submenu:
            windows: Switch Change size Zoom

F3   For retrieving files to edit from your floppy disk.
            Submenu:
            files: Edit different file Insert file

F4   For inserting blank lines or deleting lines in a file.
            Submenu:
            lines: Insert after insert Before Delete Undelete

F5   For finding or changing strings of characters in a file.
            Submenu:
            look: Forward find Backward find fOrward change bAckward change

F6   For moving to a particular place in a file.
            Submenu:
            goto: after executed Line Output pg

F7   To mark a block of lines in a file.
            Submenu:
            mark/unmark area of: Lines Rectangle Command

F8   To operate upon a marked block in a file.
            Submenu:
            area: Copy Move Delete Round

F9   To save a file or to delete a file from disk.
            Submenu:
            file: write Whole file Delete

F10   To run a command file or to exit to system prompt.
            Submenu:
            run: run from Cursor Exit to prompt

Figure 5.4: Main uses of the Function keys by key. (The way these facilities work is described as you work through this book.)

Note that all the F keys are available in edit mode, but when you are in menu mode you only have F1, F2, F7, F9 and F10 available. Pressing the other Function keys while in menu mode, will produce the message *Not available in menu mode* at the bottom of the screen. To remove this message, press the -Del key. (Pressing Esc does not work here). Then switch modes (Alt E) and again press the F key you want.

If you press the wrong Function key and have not pressed (R) , cancel the operation and remove the minimenu by pressing Esc on the keyboard. If you press (R) and select the wrong item, the action to take to cancel the operation is sometimes shown on the screen; Esc will often retrieve the situation.

5.9 The Help system

To obtain some on-screen help to using the system, press F1 and select the first entry: *Review help* by pressing (R). You will be shown a reminder of what the function keys do, and a guide to menu commands. If F1 is pressed again, a screen is displayed showing how to move the cursor around the file being edited. The bottom line of the screen says:

Enter command or press F1 for more help or Escape to continue.

If you enter a command by pressing the appropriate keys on the keyboard, it does NOT provide help information on that command, but invokes it. You are most likely to want Esc to return to where you were when you pressed F1.

5.10 The Glossary

SPSS/PC+ contains a glossary explaining the meaning of technical terms you may come across. These terms are concerned both with the operation of SPSS/PC+ itself, and with statistical analysis. To see a definition of a term such as *mode*, press F1 and select *Glossary* from the minimenu. A window will appear on the screen. Type in the item you want, and an explanation will be shown. To move up and down the glossary, use Ctrl PgUp or Ctrl PgDn. To remove the glossary display, press Esc.

5.11 Working from the system prompt

There is another mode for using SPSS/PC+ in addition to the menu and edit modes. If you select the option *Exit to prompt* from the minimenu obtained by pressing F10, the screen goes blank except that on the bottom line you will see:

SPSS/PC:

This is known as the system prompt, and shows you are in direct mode. In direct mode, you type in commands directly, one at a time, and press (R). SPSS/PC+ will carry out the command and then come back with the prompt, waiting for the next command. When you are experienced at using SPSS/PC+ you may find that using this direct mode of interacting with the program is easier than using menus or using the scratchpad in Review (SPSS/PC+'s editor), but beginners are advised to avoid it.

If you find yourself faced with the system prompt, get back into Review by typing:

`Review.`

Do not forget the full stop! Press (R) and you will then get back into Review, and be faced with a screen like Fig 5.1 except that the scratchpad may contain entries.

5.12 Leaving SPSS/PC+

There are two major methods for leaving SPSS/PC+. If you are in menu mode, start at step 1 in the list below; if you are in edit mode start at step 4.

1 In menu mode, move the cursor to the *FINISH* command at the bottom of the menu

2 Press (R) to select that command. It will be pasted into the scratchpad (the bottom half of the screen)

3 Go to step 6

4 In edit mode, type the word: `finish.` into the scratchpad. Make sure you put a full stop after the word. (All SPSS/PC+ commands must end in a full stop.)

5 Go to step 6

6 Ensure the cursor is on the line containing the word 'finish', and press F10. A minimenu will appear on the bottom line of the screen, with two entries:

run from Cursor   Exit to prompt

(If you do not have this minimenu on the bottom line, because you pressed some key other than F10, press the Esc key and then press F10.) The *run from Cursor* entry will be highlighted (dark on light). This is the option required

7 Press (R)

SPSS/PC+ will obey the command `finish.`, and the system will return to DOS.

The sequence F10 followed by (R) is always used to run the instructions shown in the scratchpad.

You have now run your first SPSS/PC+ command! But to do anything worthwhile you must start with a data file, covered in Chapter 6.

The Data File

6.1 What the data file is

The data file is simply the stored record of the numbers (data) which are to be analysed. The data can be kept in the same file as the commands which tell SPSS/PC+ how the data is organised and what analysis to do, but I recommend that you keep them separate. For beginners, it is simpler to think of the data and the commands as separate and to support this conceptual distinction by keeping them physically distinct. (An example of how the data and commands can be saved in one file is shown in Figure 9.2 in Section 9.6)

6.2 The data file used in this book

In explaining how to use SPSS/PC+, one set of data is going to be used throughout the rest of this book. The amount of data is small, but once you have learned to use SPSS/PC+ on a small set, there should be no problems with a much larger set since the principles are the same.

Imagine that we have carried out a piece of research on a group of salespeople. We gave a questionnaire to 22 salespeople from three different employers, and each respondent was asked their sex, the name of their employer, the area of the country they work in (either North or South), and then three questions intended to reveal their attitude towards their job. Each of these questions (numbers 5-7 in Figure 6.1) invited a response on a scale from 1 to 5. The questionnaire also asked the number of customers each salesperson had visited during the previous month, their total sales for the previous month and the date they started working for their company. Figure 6.1 shows an example of a completed questionnaire from one respondent, and in all there are 22 questionnaires like this.

Where there are alternative answers, please underline the one
relevant to you. For the other questions, please fill in your
answer.

                                          Respondent number: 01

1 What is your name?   K Smith

2 Are you male or female?   (1) M   (2) F

3 What is the name of your employer?
   (1) Jones and Sons   (2) Smith and Company   (3) Tomkins

4 In which area of the country do you work?   (1) North (2) South

Please indicate your reponse to the following three questions by
underlining one of the numbers, using the following scale:
   1 means that you strongly agree with the statement;
   2 that you agree with it;
   3 that you are uncertain;
   4 that you disagree;
   5 that you strongly disagree with the statement.

5 In general I enjoy my job   1   2   3   4   5

6 In my company, hard work gets rewards 1   2   3   4   5

7 I often wish I was doing a different job 1   2   3   4   5

8 How many customers did you visit last month?   43

9 What was your total sales value last month?   3450.60

10 Enter the date you started working for your present employer:
                              01 day 06 month 88 yr

Figure 6.1 Completed Sales Personnel Questionnaire

When encoding these responses for SPSS/PC+, transform all the responses into numbers. (SPSS/PC+ can deal with responses that are coded as letters or words, see Section 24.2; but there are drawbacks so whenever possible just use numbers.) Although the respondents tell us they are male or female, express the answer as a number; we shall use 1 to represent male and 2 to represent female. Similarly, we shall give each employer a number and record the respondent's employer as 1, 2 or 3; the value 1 is used to represent Jones and Sons. The area of work is also coded numerically with 1 for North and 2 for South.

Although this type of investigation may not be of any interest to you, the kind of responses obtained are similar to those yielded by many kinds of research. Essentially, we have various types of numbers. Here they are used to represent sex, employer, area of country, attitude expressed on three questions, two performance measures (customers visited and sales), and the date when the person started with the company. We could have data on socio-economic status, number of children, or a thousand other things which can be represented as numbers.

The first thing to do in preparing the data for SPSS/PC+ is to lay out the data for each respondent in a consistent order, in a line like this:

```
01 2 1 1 4 5 1 043 03450.60 010688
```

The first numbers (01) are the respondent identification number; it is useful to give every respondent a unique identifying number and start the line of data with it. This helps later if you need to check the data (and you almost certainly will!) The third number (2) represents the respondent's sex, with 1 meaning male and 2 meaning female. The next 1 is the code number of the employer, and the following 1 shows the respondent was working in the North. The sequence 4 5 1 is the response to the three attitude questions (questions 5, 6 and 7), while 043 is the number of customers visited. 03450.60 is the sales, and the last set of numbers is the date of starting at the company expressed as day, month and year.

6.3 General features of a data file

Table 6.1 shows the complete set of data for the 22 respondents in our survey. Each line of the file is a case (usually each line is the data from one subject), and it is essential that the data for each respondent, known as a case, is laid out in the same sequence. (In Table 6.1, the data for the respondent is in the same order as they appear on the data sheet; this is not necessary, but is usually the most convenient way of arranging things.)

The second point to note is that it is essential that if an item of data occupies two columns for one respondent it must occupy two columns for every respondent. For example, you cannot indicate the first day of the month as a 1 for some people and the 10th day as 10 for others; you must always use two columns to indicate day of month. This is why the leading zeroes are included in the dates, and 1st June 1988 is written as 010688. (You can omit the leading zeroes and have a blank column instead, but this confuses the appearance of the data and makes it easier to make mistakes, so insert the leading zeroes!)

Table 6.1: The data used in this book laid out in SPSS/PC+ style

---

```
01 2 1 1 4 5 1 043 03450.60 010688
02 1 2 2 4 4 3 046 04984.42 080690
03 1 1 2 2 3 5 048 10432.82 090690
04 1 3 1 2 3 4 083 08235.21 010690
05 3 2 2 2 2 4 071 06441.38 080690
06 2 3 2 3 3 3 072 06497.05 090690
07 2 1 2 3 2 5 042 03835.26 010690
08 1 2 2 4 5 3 028 03819.00 080690
09 1 1 1 2 3 4 041 05723.52 090690
10 1 3 2 1 2 5 076 07937.45 080690
11 2 2 1 2 3 3 039 04582.44 090690
12 1 1 1 2 3 4 030 02005.30 010690
13 1 3 2 2 2 4 068 08914.50 030691
14 2 2 2 1 2 4 033 03124.20 050691
15 2 2 2 5 4 1 036 04222.45 030691
16 2 3 1 2 2 4 079 08881.28 310591
17 1 1 2 3 4 3 038 03449.35 050691
18 2 1 1 2 3 4 048 07882.60 310591
19 2 3 1 4 3 1 058 08779.00 030691
20 2 2 2 1 3 4 060 05822.68 310591
21 1 2 2 3 4 3 039 04004.80 030691
22 2 1 1 2 3 3 040 05886.40 050690
```

The data must be in the same columns for all cases (respondents). If column 4 contains the sex of respondent 1, the same column must contain that data for all the other respondents. (This is not strictly necessary, but I strongly recommend you use this consistent spacing style because it does make it much easier to check your data file if you ever need to do so... as you probably will!)

In Table 6.1 the numbers are laid out in series separated by blanks; this is not necessary, and the data for respondent 1 could be written as:

```
0121145104303450.60010688
```

This is definitely not recommended: you may need to check your data later, and it is much easier to do so if the figures are divided into short sequences rather than being one uninterrupted line.

Where there is a lengthy set of data for each respondent, it will be too long to fit onto one line. This is not a problem, the data can just continue on the next line. The data shown in Table 6.1 could have been laid out like this:

```
01 2 1 1 4 51043
   03450.60 010688
02 1 2 244 3 046
   04984.42 080690
```

and so on.

The indentation of the second line for each case is not necessary, but I recommend that you do indent because it does make it much easier to check your data file should you ever need to do so. Remember to be consistent for every case (respondent). If the data extends over two lines, the command file must indicate that this is so, as explained in Section 9.5.

6.4 Writing the data file

To write the data as a file that can be analysed later, proceed as follows:

❑ Get into SPSS/PC+ and put your floppy disk into the drive

❑ Get into Edit mode by pressing Alt E

❑ Type in the lines of data as shown in Table 6.1, pressing (R) at the end of each line *except the last one*. Start each line in column 1, and use the exact spacing shown in Table 6.1, with one blank column between items of data.

❑ When the last line is typed in, do not press (R) , but save the file, as described in Section 7.1. Call the file exdat.

If you make a mistake when typing in, refer to chapter 8 for an explanation of how to correct errors when typing in and how to edit a file that has been saved.

You have now written a data file and saved it on the floppy disk. The next task is to write the command file which informs SPSS/PC+ of the structure of the data file and instructs it what analyses to perform on the data. How to create the command file is described in Chapter 9.

7

Saving and Retrieving Files from the Floppy Disk

7.1 Saving a file

To save a file, proceed as follows:

❏ Press F9 and a minimenu will appear on the bottom line of the screen. The option *write Whole file* will be highlighted

❏ To select this option press (R) and a box will appear at the bottom of the screen, inviting you to type in a name for the file.

❏ Type in a:filename (R)

The a: writes the file to the floppy disk. Use whatever name you want the file to be called in place of filename, for example: a:exdat. It is sensible to give a data file a name ending in *dat* so you know whenever you see a list of files that this is a data file.

When the file has been saved, the message *done (including nn lines from memory)* appears at the bottom left of the screen.

When saving a revised version of an existing file which has been retrieved from disk, it is not necessary to type in the file name, as it will be offered in the window at the bottom of the screen when F9 (R) has been keyed in. So you can just press (R). The revised version will then replace the previous version on the floppy disk. Of course to keep the old version and the revised version, type in a new filename when saving the revised version.

The file is now stored on the floppy disk (drive A). One annoying feature is that although the file has been saved as exdat, you are still actually editing the scratchpad, and that is the name of the current file shown in the bottom right of the screen. You can check that the file has indeed been stored on the floppy by using the procedure for viewing the list of files on the floppy described in Section 7.4.

7.2 Filenames

A filename cannot be longer than eight characters plus a full stop plus three letters for the filename extension. So *exerc.dat* is acceptable, and so is *exercdat*. But *exercise1dat* will be shortened to the first eight characters and will be *exercise*.

7.3 Retrieving a file from disk

To retrieve a file that has been stored on the floppy disk, follow these steps:

❑ Ensure you are in edit mode

❑ Press F3 and a minimenu will appear on the bottom line of the screen. The first entry, *Edit different file* is highlighted.

❑ To select this entry press (R) . A box will appear at the bottom of the screen, inviting you to type in the name of the file to edit.

❑ Type in a:filename (R)

Remember to use the real file name in place of filename. If the filename has an extension (e.g. spss.lis), the complete name, including the extension, must be typed in.

The file will be retrieved and appear in the scratchpad, with the filename given on the bottom right of the screen.

7.4 Finding out what is on the floppy disk

When you have forgotten the name of the file you want to retrieve from the floppy disk, SPSS/PC+ will display a list of all the files on the floppy if you proceed as follows:

❑ Press F1

❑ Move the cursor along the minimenu at the bottom of the screen until it is over *File list* and press (R) . A typing window will appear on the bottom line of the screen, asking for a File specification.

❑ To indicate that the files on the floppy disk (drive A) should be listed, type:
    a: (R)

A list of the files on the floppy is shown in the top half of the screen. The first file in the list is highlighted, and details of its size and creation date are shown in a window just above the centre of the screen. When the cursor is moved over the list of filenames using the cursor-movement keys, details of the file highlighted are shown in the window. To remove the list press Esc.

7.5 Deleting a file from the floppy disk

To delete a file, follow these instructions:

❑ Press F9 and a minimenu will appear on the bottom line of the screen.

❑ Move the cursor so it is over the entry *Delete.*

❑ To select this option press (R). A box will appear at the bottom of the screen, inviting you to type in the name of the file to be deleted.

❑ Type in a:filename (R) and the named file will be deleted from the floppy disk.

An alternative procedure is to leave SPSS/PC+, and delete the file called filename from the floppy using the DOS command:

del a: filename(R)

Correcting Errors in a File

8.1 Correcting errors when typing in

To correct errors, put the cursor over the character or space after the error and press the -Del key, or put the cursor over the error and press the number/Del key: the wrong character will then be removed and the correct figure can be typed in.

At the bottom of the screen, toward the right hand edge, there is a window with the letters *Ins*, indicating Insert mode. When a new number is typed in, it will be inserted at the cursor position and the rest of the line will shift right to make room for it.

You can switch between Insert and Overtype modes by pressing the Ins key on the keyboard. When in Overtype mode, the *Ins* on the bottom line of the screen disappears. Now if the cursor is positioned in the centre of a line and a new number keyed in, it will replace the number that was there before, rather than making extra room for the new number.

Moving the cursor in the file is speeded up by using Ctrl left-arrow or Ctrl right-arrow, which take the cursor to the start or end of the line. Pressing the Home key moves it to the top of the window, Ctrl Home to the first line of the file.

8.2 Editing a file stored on the floppy disk

To alter (edit) a file stored on the floppy disk, follow these steps:

❑ If necessary, retrieve the file from the disk as described in Section 7.3

❑ Make the changes required

❑ Save the file as explained in Section 7.1.

When a file has been edited, the revised version can be saved under the original name or under a different one. If it is saved with the original name, the revised version will overwrite the original. If a new name is used, the old version and the new version will both be kept.

8.3 Inserting blank lines in a file

To insert a blank line in a file:

❑ Move the cursor to the line above or below the point where the blank line is to be inserted

❑ Press F4 and a menu appears at the bottom of the screen

❑ Move the cursor so it is over *Insert after* or *insert Before*, whichever is appropriate

❑ Press (R) . A blank line will appear above or below the line at which the cursor was positioned when F4 was pressed.

8.4 Removing lines from a file

To remove a single whole line from the file:

❑ Move the cursor so it is on the line to be deleted

❑ Press F4 and a menu appears at the bottom of the screen

❑ Move the menu cursor until it is over *Delete*

❑ Press (R) and the line will be removed.

To remove a set of successive lines (known as a block):

❑ Mark the block, as explained in Section 8.5

❑ Press F8 and a menu appears at the bottom of the screen

❑ Move the menu cursor until it is over *Delete*

❑ Press (R) and the marked block will be deleted.

8.5 Marking a block of lines

❑ Put the cursor on the first line of the block to be marked

❑ Press F7 and a minimenu appears along the bottom of the screen. The first entry is *Lines*

❑ To select this press (R) . The line in the file will flash

❑ Move the cursor to the last line of the block to be marked

❑ Press F7 and the block of lines will be highlighted.

❑ If you make a mistake marking a block, cancel the marking by pressing F7 again.

8.6 Joining lines

If you have the cursor in the middle of a line and press (R), the part after the cursor will become a new line. Frequently this is not what was intended! To join the line back to its root, put the cursor at the end of upper line and press the number/Del key on the keypad (not the Del key on the main part of the keyboard).

8.7 Moving lines

To move one line in a file:

❑ Go through the procedure for deleting the line described in Section 8.4

❑ Move the cursor to the line below the position where you want the line to be inserted

❑ Press F4

❑ Select the entry *Undelete* from the minimenu on the bottom line of the screen

❑ Press (R) and the line will be inserted above the line on which the cursor rested when (R) was pressed.

To move a block of lines:

❑ Mark the block as described in Section 8.5

❑ Move the cursor so it is at the position where the marked block is to appear

❑ Press F8

❑ Select the minimenu entry *Move*

❑ Press (R) and the marked block will be moved to the new location.

8.8 Saving some lines as a separate file

When a block of lines has been marked, as described in Section 8.5, it can be saved as a separate file:

❑ Mark the block of lines

❑ Press F9. The minimenu contains a new option: *write Marked area*

❑ Move the cursor so it is over this entry

❑ To select it, press (R) and a window appears asking for the filename to be used when the block is saved

❑ Type in the filename, preceding it with a : to have the file stored on the floppy disk

❑ Press (R) .

8.9 Removing or moving columns

When editing a file of data containing columns of figures, you can remove or move some columns of numbers. In practice, this is very rarely necessary, but can be done using the Rectangle function from the F7 key:

❑ Position the cursor over the top left corner of the block to be marked

❑ Press F7

❑ Position the cursor over *Rectangle* in the minimenu on the bottom line of the screen

❑ Move the cursor to the bottom right corner of the rectangular block

❑ Press F7. The area marked will be highlighted.

❑ If the rectangle is being moved, put the cursor at the new location for the block

❑ Press F8 and a minimenu appears on the bottom of the screen

❑ Move the cursor so it is over *Move* or *Delete*, whichever is appropriate

❑ Press (R) .

8.10 Saving some columns of data as a separate file

To create a data file containing just some of the columns of data from the original file:

❑ Mark a rectangular block as described in Section 8.9 above

❑ Press F9

❑ Select the option *write Marked area* from the minimenu by putting the cursor over it

❑ Press (R) and a typing window appears at the bottom of the screen

❑ Type in the name for the new file

❑ Press (R) .

8.11 Obtaining a clean, empty file to write to

To get a clean, new file (for example to write your first Command File), proceed as follows:

❑ Ensure you are in edit mode (Alt E)

❑ Press F3. At the bottom of the screen the cursor will be over a minimenu entry *Edit different file*.

❑ To select this entry press (R) . A typing window titled *File to edit* appears at the bottom of the screen

❑ Type in the name of the new file: a:fn (R), remembering to use the name you want in place of fn .

The scratchpad will be cleared and you have a new file to write to. The file is called whatever you used instead of fn, and the name is shown at the bottom right of the screen.

9

The Command File

9.1 What the command file is

The file exdat holds the data to be analysed. You now have to write the command file. This contains the instructions which tell SPSS/PC+ about the data in the data file (data definition commands), where the output from the analysis is to go (operation commands), and what analysis SPSS/PC+ is to perform (procedure commands).

These instructions have to be entered into the command file in a particular form and in a proper order. The order is as you would expect. For example, you must explain which data file to use before you order the program to analyse the figures. Similarly, it is no good telling the program to compare the scores of males and females if you have not already told it that the data for sex is in column 4 of the data file.

The data definition section of the Command File tells SPSS/PC+:

❑ Where the data file is

❑ The way the data is laid out in the data file (e.g. that the data in column 4 indicates the respondent's sex)

❑ The names of the variables included in the data file (e.g. that the data in column 4 is to be referred to as sex, gender or whatever name you want to give it).

In exdat we have data on the following variables: id number, sex, employer, area, attitude questions 1, 2 and 3, customers visited, sales, date started job. But these names cannot be used, because within SPSS/PC+ a variable name cannot contain a blank space (so id number is not acceptable), and must be no more than eight characters long. So names that fit these rules must be used.

Obviously it is better to use names that are informative. Names like `var1`, `var2` and the like can be confusing later. So use names that are recognisably related to the 'real-life' names of the variables. For exdat, these might be: `id`, `sex`, `employer`, `area`, `att1`, `att2`, `att3`, `cust`, `sales` and `datest` (for date started job). There is a special command (YRMODA, covered in Section 19.8) for dealing with dates which needs the year, month and day of a date to be listed separately. So we shall divide the date of starting the job into three components: `dstd`, `dstm` and `dsty` for day, month and year.

9.2 Command file example 1 (excom1)

You are going to create the very simple Command File, shown in Figure 9.1, that will enable you to analyse the data stored in exdat.

Note that all command lines must end in a full-stop. In Figure 9.1, the line beginning DATA LIST FILE occupies three lines of screen and paper, but is one SPSS/PC+ command line which ends with `dsty 33-34`.

```
DATA LIST FILE 'a:exdat' FIXED /id 1-2 sex 4 employer 6 area 8
    att1 10 att2 12 att3 14 cust 16-18 sales 20-27 (2) dstd 29-30
    dstm 31-32 dsty 33-34.
SET /LISTING 'a:ex1.lis'.
LIST.
```

Figure 9.1: The command file excom1

The DATA LIST FILE line is essential. The first part DATA LIST FILE `'a:exdat'` tells the program to get the data for analysis from the file exdat which is in drive A (the floppy disk). The second part of this line, FIXED `/id 1-2 sex 4` etc tells the program how the data in each row of the data file is laid out: `id` is in columns 1-2, `sex` in column 4, `employer` in column 6 and so on. `Sales` are in columns 20 to 27; the (2) indicates that there are two decimal places in these figures. The manual states that it is not necessary to specify that numbers are decimals if the decimal point is keyed in, but problems can occur if this specification is omitted.

The SET / LISTING `'a:ex1.lis'`. line tells the program to send the output to a file called ex1.lis on drive A (the floppy disk). If this instruction is not included, the output will go to a file called SPSS.LIS on drive C.

The last line, LIST. is an example of a PROCEDURES command. These instruct
SPSS/PC+ to carry out some analysis on the data. Much of the rest of this book will
be concerned with explaining what the various procedures do. LIST tells SPSS/PC+
to list the data. It is useful when first creating a new command file because it lets you
check that the program is reading the data file correctly, and has understood your
commands about the way the data is laid out.

So this is a (very simple) complete Command File. The question is, how do you
create it? There are two different ways. One way is to be in the edit mode and type
all the lines into the scratchpad. The other way is to use the menu system.

9.3 Creating the Command File excom1 with the menu system

To write the Command File, start with a 'clean', new file; it is like starting on a fresh
sheet of paper. Do NOT simply add the Command File lines to the Data File; it will
not work! To get a clean, new file to write your Command File, follow the
instructions given in Section 8.11, using as the name of the new Command File:
a:excom1. The a: tells SPSS/PC+ to store the file on the floppy disk (drive A); the
name of the file is excom1.

The scratchpad will be cleared, providing a new file to write to. The name of the new
file, excom1, will be shown on the bottom line of the screen.

To create the command file lines, get into menu mode, put the cursor over the
appropriate line in the menu and press (R). The menu entry is then pasted into the
scratchpad. At certain points, information has to be typed in from the keyboard.

To get the first line of the Command File, proceed as follows:

❑ Make sure you are in menu mode and that the first-level main menu (headed *MAIN
MENU)* is in the top left of the screen

❑ Move the cursor down so it is over the entry *read or write data*

❑ Press the right arrow key to enter the submenu

❑ Move the cursor to the *DATA LIST* entry

❑ Press (R) to paste *DATA LIST* into the scratchpad. The submenu of *DATA LIST*
will automatically be shown in the screen's menu area

❑ Move the cursor to *FILE''*

❏ Press (R) to paste *FILE''* into the scratchpad. A window appears in the centre of the screen

❏ Type in the filename a:exdat (R). Remember to include the a: since this tells the program the file is on the floppy, and do not put a full-stop at the end as this is already included by the system

❏ Move the cursor in the menu so it is over *FIXED*

❏ Press (R) to paste *FIXED* into the scratchpad. The cursor will move to *numeric variables* in a submenu

❏ Press Alt T to enter type-in mode

❏ Type in the following details on the layout of the data:

```
id 1-2 sex 4 employer 6 area 8 att1 10 att2 12 att3 14 cust 16-18 sales
20-27 (2) dstd 29-30 dstm 31-32 dsty 33-34
```

You will have to press (R) before the input gets to the right edge of the window, as you cannot type in a line longer than the window's length. When you press (R), the material you have typed in is pasted into the scratchpad. Press Alt T again to bring the typing window back, and key in the rest of the line. When you reach the end of the line (dsty 33-34), do not put a full-stop; just press (R)

All this takes much longer to describe than to do, once you know what you are supposed to be doing! If you find you have pressed the wrong key at any stage, refer to Section 9.4 below.

You should have in the scratchpad a line which is the same as the first line in Figure 9.1. If you are having problems, see Section 9.4.

To write the SET /LISTING line, first check that you are still in menu mode, with the cursor in the scratchpad immediately before the full stop at the end of the DATA LIST FILE line you have just written. If the cursor is not located there, go into edit mode (Alt E), and use the arrow keys to position the scratchpad cursor at the end of the DATA LIST FILE line. Get back into menu mode (Alt E again), and follow these steps:

❏ Press Ctrl Escape, to move to the first level of the main menu

❏ Move the cursor down until it is over the entry *session control & info*

❏ Press the right arrow key. The cursor will be over the entry *SET* in the submenu

❏ Press the right arrow key again to reveal a submenu

❏ Bring the cursor down until it is over *output* and press the right arrow key. You will see yet another submenu, and the eighth entry down the list is */LISTING*.

❏ Move the cursor down until it is over */LISTING* and press the right arrow key. This will reveal another submenu, and the cursor will be over ''

❏ Press (R) . *SET /LISTING* ''. is added to the scratchpad file, and a typing window appears in the centre of the screen

❏ Type in (without a final full stop) a:ex1.lis and press (R) .

The scratchpad line will now be SET /LISTING `a:ex1.lis'.

Note: Every time this command file is run, the output will be sent to ex1.lis. If it is run twice, without leaving SPSS/PC+, the second set of outputs will be added on to the end of ex1.lis. But if you leave SPSS/PC+ and then start it again from the DOS level by using SPSSPC (R), on the next run a new version of ex1.lis will be created. This will OVERWRITE the first - you will have lost the results of your first analysis.

To overcome this, there are two alternatives. One method is to alter the output filename in the SET /LISTING line every time you enter SPSS/PC+, before you run a command file. When creating a second command file (excom2), the output file will be changed to ex2.LIS, so that running that command file does not overwrite ex1.lis. The second method for ensuring ex1.LIS is preserved is to change its name after leaving SPSS/PC+, using the DOS rename command, as explained in Section 3.11.

The last line, LIST . is obtained as follows:

❏ Press Ctrl Escape to go back to the first level main menu

❏ Move the cursor so it is over *analyze data*

❏ Press the right arrow key to reveal a submenu

❏ Move the cursor down so it is over *reports and tables*

Press the right arrow key again. You will now see another submenu, and the first entry, which has the cursor over it, is *LIST*.

❏ Press (R) to paste *LIST*. into the scratchpad.

Assuming the command file is as shown in Figure 9.1, save it as described in Section 7.1, i.e. press F9 (R) and (R) again. The file is now saved on the floppy as excom1.

The data file, exdat, and the command file, excom1, are now stored on the floppy disk. The next task is to tell SPSS/PC+ to run the command file. How to do this is described in Chapter 10.

9.4 If you run into problems

There is a danger that the complexity of this task will overwhelm you; for the beginner, creating the lines of the command file seems a very complicated and laborious business. But do persevere: after a little practice you will find it is much easier than it looks now.

Remember to look at the Help window in the upper right of the screen; it offers you useful information about the commands that are highlighted in the menu and sometimes provides examples of what command lines should look like.

If you find that you are not where you want to be in the menu system, you can always move up a level by pressing the left arrow key, or can jump to the top level menu by pressing Ctrl Esc.

If you make an error when typing into the typing window, you can edit it using the usual procedure of moving the cursor within the window, deleting characters, inserting characters in the middle of a line and so on. To remove the typing window and not have its contents pasted into the scratchpad, press the Esc key; get the window back with Alt T.

As you try to create the command lines, you may obtain some lines that you know are wrong. Do not worry, they can easily be removed later using the technique described in Section 8.4 of putting the cursor on the faulty line, pressing F4 and selecting the *Delete* option.

If all else fails, you can get into edit mode (Alt E) and type in the command lines from the keyboard. But you can make more mistakes this way; you may make a lot of mistakes with the menu system, but it does not let you make some real howlers!

Be careful when you are typing in information; you do NOT need to type full-stops at the ends of lines when using the menu system, as they are generated automatically. Look at the screen to see if you have inadvertently obtained two full-stops at the end of a line. If so, you can edit the file to remove one of them, by getting into edit mode, moving the cursor so it is over the second full stop and pressing the -Del/ key.

If you end up in real chaos and want to start again, the easiest thing to do is go through the procedure of obtaining a new file to write to (Section 8.11). So long as you have not saved your chaotic attempt at creating the command file, you can as before call the new file a:excom1. When you press F3 and select *Edit different file* from the minimenu, the program will tell you (on the bottom line of the screen) that there are unsaved changes in the file you are writing, and ask if it is alright to leave it. Press y (for yes) and (R). The system will then give you another clean file called a:excom1, and you can have another try.

If you have saved an error-filled version of excom1 and want to delete it before beginning again, follow the procedure described in Section 7.5.

9.5 If the data occupies more than one line in the data file

The example data used in this book occupies one line per case (respondent). Real data may be longer and occupy two lines of the data file. In such a case, it is necessary to tell SPSS/PC+ to read data from the second line for each case, by separating the two lines with / in the DATA LIST FILE line. For example, suppose each case in exdat had been written as follows, with two lines per respondent, the first line ending with the data on att3:

```
01 2 1 1 4 5 1
   043 03450.60 010688
02 1 2 2 4 4 3
   046 04984.42 080690
........
```

The second line starts with the data on customers visited (cust). The DATA LIST line in the command file would have to be written like this:

```
DATA LIST FILE 'a:exdat' FIXED /id 1-2 sex 4 employer 6 area 8
   att1 10 att2 12 att3 14 /cust 16-18 sales 20-27 (2)
   dstd 29-30 dstm 31-32 dsty 33-34.
```

The / in the list of variables, after the description of att3, tells SPSS/PC+ to go to the next line to read the next variable (cust).

9.6 Data and command files combined

The command file and data files are kept separate in this book, because it easier to explain the way SPSS/PC+ operates if you think of them as separate. But they can be amalgamated, as shown in Figure 9.2. Note that the order of the various parts is vital.

Do NOT copy this file - it is only an example!!!

```
TITLE 'Example data+command files'.
DATA LIST FIXED /id 1-2 sex 4 age 6-7.
VALUE LABELS sex 1 'male' 2 'female'.
MISSING VALUE sex(3).
SET /LISTING 'a:\myd.lis'.
BEGIN DATA.
01 1 20
02 1 15
........
19 3 19
END DATA.
FREQUENCIES /VARIABLES sex.
FINISH.
```

Figure 9.2: Example of a data file and command file amalgamated.

9.7 Running a DOS command from SPSS/PC+

DOS commands can be run without leaving SPSS/PC+. To insert a DOS command (such as `del a:ex.lis`, which deletes the ex.lis file from the floppy disk) into a command file, follow this procedure:

❏ Select run *DOS or other pgms* from the main menu

❏ Press the right arrow key to move to the submenu

❏ To paste *DOS* into the scratchpad, ensure the cursor is over it and press (R) . A typing window appears

❏ Type in the DOS command and press (R) .

When the command file is run, it will execute this single DOS instruction and then continue with the other SPSS/PC+ commands.

10

Running SPSS/PC+

10.1 How to Invoke SPSS/PC+

The floppy disk now contains the data file (exdat) and the command file. The next step is to tell SPSS/PC+ to apply the commands in the command file to the data. There are two ways of doing this.

Method 1

1a) Make sure the floppy containing the data and command files is in the disk drive

1b) If the command file is in the scratchpad go to step 1g

1c) Ensure you are in edit mode

1d) Press F3

1e) To select *Edit diff file* press (R)

1f) To bring excom1 into the scratchpad, type:
```
a:excom1 (R)
```

1g) Press Ctrl Home to position the cursor on the first line of the file

1h) Press F10 and a minimenu appears on the bottom line of the screen. There are two options, and the first one, *run from Cursor*, is highlighted.

1i) To invoke this command press (R) .

Method 2

2a) Make sure the floppy containing the data and command files is in the disk drive

2b) Ensure the scratchpad is empty. If it is not, delete the lines using the procedure described in Section 8.4

2c) Ensure you are in edit mode

2d) Type INCLUDE `a:excom1`. Remember the full stop!

2e) Leave the cursor on this line or move the cursor so it is on this line. Press F10 and a minimenu appears on the bottom line of the screen. There are two options, and the first one, *run from Cursor*, is highlighted

2d) Press (R).

With either technique, SPSS/PC+ will try to follow the commands in the command file. The screen shows what is happening: the system lists the commands as it comes to them and writes the results of the commands on the screen. At various times it will stop, and the word *MORE* will appear in the top right of the screen. Press any key on the keyboard and the program will go on to the next stage.

If all is well, the program will follow the commands, and display the table illustrated in Figure 10.1. When a key is pressed at the last *MORE* sign, it will return to the original entry screen.

If all is not well, the program will stop trying to run the command file; a message indicating the problem will be shown and the entry screen will re-appear. (If Method 1 of invoking the run was used, the scratchpad will be empty. If Method 2 was used, the scratchpad will contain the INCLUDE `a:excom1`. command.) Do not worry: this is a very common event! See Section 10.3 if the run has failed.

When the analysis is complete, the floppy will contain the output file, ex1.lis. If you have followed the instructions given here, you are still in SPSS/PC+ and faced with the entry screen. There are easy ways of looking at the output file without leaving SPSS/PC+ (see Chapter 11), but for the moment return to DOS following the procedure described in Section 5.12, and examine the output file from there.

10.2 Examining the output of excom1

From the DOS level, inspect the contents of the output file ex1.lis by typing:

```
type a:ex1.lis (R)
```

```
LIST.
The raw data or transformation pass is proceeding
     22 cases are written to the uncompressed active file.
------------------------------------------------------------------------
Page    2                            SPSS/PC+                    10/8/91

ID SEX EMPLOYER AREA ATT1 ATT2 ATT3 CUST     SALES DSTD DSTM DSTY

  1   2      1    1    4    5    1   43   3450.60    1    6   88
  2   1      2    2    4    4    3   46   4984.42    8    6   90
  3   1      1    2    2    3    5   48  10432.82    9    6   90
  4   1      3    1    2    3    4   83   8235.21    1    6   90
  5   3      2    2    2    2    4   71   6441.38    8    6   90
  6   2      3    2    3    3    3   72   6497.05    9    6   90
  7   2      1    2    3    2    5   42   3835.26    1    6   90
  8   1      2    2    4    5    3   28   3819.00    8    6   90
  9   1      1    1    2    3    4   41   5723.52    9    6   90
 10   1      3    2    1    2    5   76   7937.45    8    6   90
 11   2      2    1    2    3    3   39   4582.44    9    6   90
 12   1      1    1    2    3    4   30   2005.30    1    6   90
 13   1      3    2    2    2    4   68   8914.50    3    6   91
 14   2      2    2    1    2    4   33   3124.20    5    6   91
 15   2      2    2    5    4    1   36   4222.45    3    6   91
 16   2      3    1    2    2    4   79   8881.28   31    5   91
 17   1      1    2    3    4    3   38   3449.35    5    6   91
 18   2      1    1    2    3    4   48   7882.60   31    5   91
 19   2      3    1    4    3    1   58   8779.00    3    6   91
 20   2      2    2    1    3    4   60   5822.68   31    5   91
 21   1      2    2    3    4    3   39   4004.80    3    6   91
------------------------------------------------------------------------
Page    3                            SPSS/PC+                    10/8/91

ID SEX EMPLOYER AREA ATT1 ATT2 ATT3 CUST     SALES DSTD DSTM DSTY

 22   2      1    1    2    3    3   40   5886.40    5    6   90


Number of cases read =       22   Number of cases listed =       22
------------------------------------------------------------------------
Page    4                            SPSS/PC+                    10/8/91

This procedure was completed at 17:26:24
------------------------------------------------------------------------
Page    5                            SPSS/PC+                    10/8/91

FINISH.

End of Include file.
```

Figure 10.1: The output (ex1.lis) from running excoml

Do not forget to type in the word type! The file ex1.lis will be presented on the screen. It scrolls up, and to make it pause press Ctrl S; restart the scrolling by pressing Ctrl S again.

To obtain a printed copy of ex1.lis, type:

```
type a:ex1.lis>prn (R)
```

If the run of excom1 was successful, the output file looks like Figure 10.1. The commands that were carried out are listed, as are the results of the commands. In this simple first example SPSS/PC+ carried out the LIST procedure which gives a listing of the data in a table that shows the variable names at the head of the columns.

You have now succeeded in 'driving' SPSS/PC+: you have written and saved a data file, written and saved a command file, had the program apply the commands to the data and create an output .LIS file. Of course it may seem rather a lot of effort to obtain such a small outcome, but once you understand the basic principles of driving SPSS/PC+ they apply to much larger sets of data and it is comparatively simple to obtain more complex forms of output.

As mentioned earlier, the LIST procedure is a helpful check that you have written the data and command files correctly. Do look carefully at the output and confirm that the system is reading the correct figures for the variables you have put into the data file.

Check that the table indicates there were 22 cases. You may find that your ex1.lis output indicates that there were 23 (or even more) in the data file. This is because you pressed (R) at the end of line 22, so that when the data file was saved the cursor was on line 23. Although line 23 has nothing on it, it is accepted by SPSS/PC as a case, but one with no data. You will have to edit the data file, exdat, and remove this line.

Recall the data file for editing, as explained in Sections 7.3 and 8.2. When a file is recalled, the end of the file is shown and the cursor is on the last line. If the cursor is on an empty line, remove it using F4 as described in Section 8.4. The cursor should now be on the last line (22) of the data file. If it is not, and you are still on an empty line, repeat this method for removing lines until the cursor is on the last line of figures in the data file.

Save the data file in its revised form (F9 and (R)), and then run excom1 again, using one of the methods described in Section 10.1.

Although this is a simple beginning, it demonstrates the way the menu system works, and how to use it. We now want to create a slightly longer command file, which will include additional information about the data file and will carry out a useful statistical analysis. This next stage is covered in Section 10.4.

10.3 When the run fails

If the analysis has failed, the output file will indicate why and where. A problem is usually due to an error in the command file. The error message gives you a clue as to what the problem might be. For example, you may have made a mistake by naming a variable in the DATA LIST line and then used a different (perhaps misspelt) name in a PROCEDURE command later on. You will then have to get back into SPSS/PC+, correct the command file and run SPSS/PC+ again.

To edit excom1, see Chapter 8. Editing is most easily done from the edit mode rather than the menu mode. When any corrections to excom1 have been made, make sure it is saved: F9, (R), (R), and run it by moving the cursor to the top line, pressing F10 and (R).

Sometimes there is an error in the data file. This can be harder to spot, because the program will tell you that it could not run a command but it is not always clear that the error is in the data rather than the command file. The commonest mistake in the data file is to have typed in the letter o rather than the number 0. If there is a letter in the data file when there should have been a digit, the program will tell you: *Invalid digit read with F Format. Check your data.* This could perhaps have been phrased in a more helpful way, since it is an invalid letter rather than an invalid digit that has caused the problem! If there is an error in the data file, you need to retrieve and edit it as described in Chapter 8.

10.4 Command File example 2 (excom2)

The Command File for the second analysis of exdat is shown in Figure 10.2.

```
TITLE 'SPSS Exercise 2'.
DATA LIST FILE 'a:exdat' FIXED /id 1-2 sex 4 employer 6 area 8
    att1 10 att2 12 att3 14 cust 16-18 sales 20-27 (2)
    dstd 29-30 dstm 31-32 dsty 33-34.
SET /LISTING 'a:ex2.lis'.
VARIABLE LABELS cust 'Customer visits' dsty 'Year started'.
VALUE LABELS sex 1 'male' 2 'female' /area 1 'North' 2 'South'.
MISSING VALUE sex(3).
FREQUENCIES /VARIABLES sex area.
```

Figure 10.2: The second Command File (excom2)

The TITLE line means the title *SPSS Exercise 2* is printed at the top of each page of printout.

The DATA LIST FILE line is identical to the one in excom1. When a series of analyses are run on one set of data, keep the same DATA LIST line since the same data file is used every time.

VARIABLE LABELS tells the program the labels to use when printing out the results. Although the data in columns 16-18 is called cust, when it is printed it will have the written label *Customer visits*. Similarly, dsty will be labelled *Year started*.

VALUE LABELS has the effect of including in the printout a verbal description of the value of a variable. You need to appreciate the difference between variables and values. In exdat, sex is one of the variables, and in column 4 of exdat all the numbers are 1, 2 or 3. These numbers are the values of the sex variable, with 1 representing male, 2 denoting female, and 3 meaning we do not know the sex of that respondent. The line shown here instructs the program to give the label *male* to the value 1 of the sex variable, and *female* to the value 2 when it presents the results. Similarly, area has been coded as 1 or 2, with 1 meaning North and 2 meaning South. The second part of this line, following the /, will give the appropriate labels to these values on the variable area.

MISSING VALUE is nearly always needed. Often some respondents have not answered all the questions asked, or have failed to provide a measure on one of the variables. It is sensible (for reasons that will become clear later) to record a no-response as a particular number. When choosing a number to represent *data missing*, use a number that cannot be a genuine number for that variable. For the sex variable in exdat, 1 represents male and 2 female, so 3 can be used to indicate no response. This MISSING VALUE line tells SPSS/PC+ that a score of 3 on sex means *sex unknown*. If you wanted to define a missing value for sales, you would use a number that could not be genuine, such as -1.00.

SET /LISTING is the same as in excom1, except that it specifies a new output file: ex2.lis. This means that the file of results of the earlier analysis (ex1.lis, the output of excom1) will not be lost when excom2 is run.

FREQUENCIES invokes the FREQUENCIES procedure. This particular instruction tells SPSS/PC+ to produce frequency tables for the values of the variables sex and area. What this actually does will be clear when this command file has been run.

10.5 Creating the second command file (excom2)

The simple method of writing excom2 is to edit excom1. Enter SPSS/PC+ and retrieve excom1 from the floppy as described in Section 7.3. It will be listed in the scratchpad. Move the cursor to the top line (be in edit mode and use the arrow keys).

The first task is to create an empty line above the first line, into which the *TITLE* command can be inserted. To do this:

❑ Ensure you are in edit mode

❑ Press F4 and select from the minimenu the option *insert Before*

❑ Press (R) and an empty line is created above the DATA LIST FILE line and the cursor moves onto it in column 1.

To create the TITLE line of excom2, it is possible to use the menus; but the simplest procedure is simply to type the line in. (In the menus, TITLE is found if you select *session control & info* from the main menu, then *titles and comments* and then the next submenu.)

The DATA LIST FILE line can be left as it is, as can SET/LISTING . . . for the moment.

To remove the LIST line:

❑ Check you are in edit mode

❑ Move the cursor so it is on the LIST line

❑ Press F4 and a minimenu appears along the bottom of the screen.

❑ Move the cursor so it is over *Delete*

❑ Press (R) .

To create the VARIABLE LABELS line:

❑ Move the cursor so it is over the full stop on the last line of the file

❑ Get back to menu mode (Alt E). *VARIABLE LABELS* is in the same menu area as the *DATA LIST* command. If you have followed these instructions the menu now shown in the menu window is the one headed */LISTING*.

❑ Press Ctrl Esc to move to Main Menu, and move cursor down to *read or write data* and go right

❑ Move the cursor down so it is over *labels and formatting*

❑ Press the right arrow key to get to the submenu. The cursor is over *VARIABLE LABELS*

❑ Press the right arrow key to show the submenu and read the Help screen: it is useful here

❑ Press (R) to paste *VARIABLE LABELS* into the scratchpad

❑ Press Alt T, which causes a typing window to appear in the centre of the screen

Type in: cust `Customer visits' dsty `Year started' (R)

The VARIABLE LABELS line should now be as shown in Figure 10.2.

To obtain the VALUE LABELS line:

❑ Move the menu cursor with the left arrow, to show the *labels and formatting* submenu

❑ Move the cursor down so it is over *VALUE LABELS*

❑ Press the right arrow key

❑ Check the cursor is over *!variables*

❑ Press (R) . *VALUE LABELS.* will be pasted into the scratchpad

❑ Use Alt T to obtain a typing window

❑ Type in: sex 1 `male' 2 `female'/ area 1 `North' 2 `South'

❑ Press (R) .

The scratchpad should now contain the line shown in Figure 10.2.

To create the MISSING VALUE line:

❑ Press left arrow key to return to the 'labels and formatting' submenu

❑ Move the cursor down so it is over *MISSING VALUE*

❑ Press right arrow key

❑ Ensure cursor is over *!variable(s)*

❑ Press (R) to paste *MISSING VALUE* into the scratchpad

❑ Press Alt T to obtain a typing window

❏ Type in sex (3)

❏ Press (R)

To create the FREQUENCIES line:

❏ Make sure the cursor is over or past the full stop at the end of the last line of the file

❏ Ensure you are in menu mode

❏ Press the left arrow key until you get to the first level of main menu

❏ Move the cursor down so it is over *analyze data*

❏ Press right arrow key to reveal the submenu

❏ Ensure the cursor is over *descriptive statistics*

❏ Press the right arrow key. Another submenu is revealed, with the cursor over *FREQUENCIES*

❏ Press the right arrow key. There is another submenu and a useful help screen

❏ Move cursor down so it is over *!/VARIABLES*

❏ Press (R) to paste *FREQUENCIES /VARIABLES* into the scratchpad

❏ Press Alt T to obtain a typing window

❏ Type in: sex area

❏ Press (R)

To change the name of the output file from ex1.lis to ex2.lis, switch to edit mode and move the cursor so it is over the full stop in ex1.lis. Press the -Del key so that ex1.lis is changed to ex.lis, with the cursor over the . and type in the number 2.

The command file in the scratchpad should now be the same as Figure 10.2. Even if it is not, save it - F9 and (R) - as excom2. If you need to make any changes, get into edit mode (Alt E), make the alterations and save the file again.

10.6 Running excom2

Run the command file excom2 by moving the cursor to the top line (Ctrl Home while in edit mode), then pressing F10 and (R) .

Watch the screen as the program runs, and try to follow what is happening. When *MORE* appears in the top right of the screen, press any key to continue the program run.

10.7 The output of excom2

If the run of excom2 has failed, you will be given some indication of what was wrong. You can then correct the command file, using the editing procedures described in Chapter 8, and run it again.

The main outcome of this run is two tables, which are reproduced in Figure 10.3. The first shows the number of cases having each value of the sex variable. The first column shows the value labels; the second the values for the variable. The third column (*Frequency*) shows the number of cases having that value for the variable.

The data file included 10 males, 11 females and 1 'missing values', the case where sex was coded as 3 because this individual had not responded to the question asking whether the respondent was male or female. Observe that the table shows that a value of 1 means male, 2 means female: this is the result of the VALUE LABELS command.

The *Percent* column shows the frequencies expressed as percentages of the total number of cases (22 in this instance).

The next column is headed *Valid Percent*. The data file has a case where the data is missing, having been given the MISSING VALUE score. So there are fewer valid cases of data on the sex variable than there are cases in the data file. SPSS/PC+ sees that there are 21, not 22 sets of data for the sex variable, and puts the percentage out of 21 (the number of valid cases) in this Valid Percent column.

The final column shows the valid percentages expressed in cumulative form. Below the table there is a statement of the number of valid cases and the number of missing cases.

The second table shows the number of cases for each area, with 9 from the North and 13 from the South. The VALUE LABELS command in excom2 ensures the table shows that 1 means North and 2 means South.

You should now be faced with the initial entry screen, and are probably wishing you could see the output file on your screen.

Chapter 11 explains how to examine the output (.LIS) file and how to edit it.

```
 SEX

                                           Valid     Cum
      Value Label     Value  Frequency  Percent Percent  Percent

 male                   1        10       45.5     47.6     47.6
 female                 2        11       50.0     52.4    100.0
                        3         1        4.5   MISSING
                                -------   -------  -------
                     TOTAL       22      100.0    100.0

 Valid Cases    21        Missing Cases    1
 ------------------------------------------------------------


 AREA

                                           Valid     Cum
      Value Label     Value  Frequency  Percent Percent  Percent

 North                  1         9       40.9     40.9     40.9
 South                  2        13       59.1     59.1    100.0
                                -------   -------  -------
                     TOTAL       22      100.0    100.0

 Valid Cases    22        Missing Cases    0
 ------------------------------------------------------------
```

Figure 10.3: The output tables from excom2 command FREQUENCIES

Exercise 10.1

Imagine you have carried out a survey of alcohol intake among young people, and have data on 1,000 respondents. For each person, you have a four-digit identification number, their age (in whole years), their sex (1 is male and 2 is female), and a measure of their weekly alcohol intake where 1 means none, 2 mean low, 3 means medium and 4 means high level of consumption. For all variables except id, -1 means the data is missing (missing values). The results of the survey have been stored in a file called alcdat on the floppy disk. The data for one respondent looks like this:

0629 17 2 2

Write a command file which would produce a table showing the number of respondents with each level of intake.

The answer is given in Appendix A.

10.8 Using Alt V to select variables

When using the menu system to create the command file, the information window frequently suggests using Alt V to produce a screen listing of the variable names that can be used to save typing them in. This will only work if the system has created an Active File i.e. you must have run SPSS/PC+ in the current session. If you are editing a command file after having run SPSS/PC+, Alt V will operate correctly. But if you have not run the program, Alt V will produce an error message: *No variables - execute a DATA LIST or TRANSLATE command.* In this case, press Esc and then use Alt T to open a typing window and key in the variable names.

The list of variables shown when Alt V is pressed includes some in addition to those defined in the DATA LIST line. These additional variables are automatically created by the program. The one you may need is $casenum, which is the system's number for the case or set of data. When the data file is read, the cases are allocated a $casenum with 1 being given to the first case read, 2 to the second and so on. For exdat, $casenum is the same as the id of each respondent, but this would not be true if the id numbers had not been in sequential order in the original data file.

11

The Output of SPSS/PC+

11.1 Examining the output (.LIS file) on screen

When SPSS/PC+ runs it creates two output files: the .LOG file and the .LIS file. The .LIS file contains the results of the analysis, and is the one of most interest. Excom2 saves the .LIS file, ex2.LIS, on the floppy disk.

As it runs, SPSS/PC+ shows on the screen the command it is executing, and the results of the command. (It is possible to suppress the screen output, but I always like to see what is going on!). When the run has finished, or is stopped because of an error in the commands, SPSS/PC+ returns to the Review mode, and the initial entry screen. You will have noticed that at the end of the run the .LIS file appears briefly in the top half of the screen but is then hidden by the menus.

To remove the menus and reveal the .LIS file, press Alt M. (To get the menus back, press Alt M again.) The end of the .LIS file is revealed in the top half of the screen. This is probably not informative, and does not show the part of the output you are interested in. To move around in the .LIS file it is necessary to move the cursor so that it is in the top half of the screen, not in the scratchpad in the bottom of the screen.

11.2 Switching the cursor to the top half of the screen

❏ Press F2; this minimenu is shown along the bottom of the screen:
Switch   Change size   Zoom

with the *Switch* option highlighted . (Note that *Zoom* may not be available, as earlier versions did not contain it.)

❑ Press (R) and the cursor will move to the bottom line of the top half of the screen.

It is helpful to have the .LIS file fill the screen, rather than just forming the top half:

❑ Press F2

❑ Select *Zoom* from the minimenu or select *Change size*

❑ Press (R) . If *Zoom* was selected, the upper window will fill the screen.

❑ If *Change size* was selected, type in the number of lines the upper window is to occupy and press (R) .

❑ Press Esc to return to the normal setting, with the scratchpad in the lower half of the screen:

❑ Press F2 and select *Switch* (R) to move the cursor back into the scratchpad.

11.3 Moving around in the screen .LIS file

The up and down arrow keys or the PgUp and PgDn keys move the cursor up or down in the file, which scrolls in the window. Ctrl left-arrow and Ctrl right-arrow move the cursor to the start and end of a line. Home moves it to the top of the window, Ctrl Home to the top of the file.

.LIS files can be lengthy, but are divided into pages. To jump to a particular page:

❑ Press F6 which reveals a window at the bottom of the screen displaying
go to: Output pg

❑ Press (R)

❑ Type in the number of the page to jump to

❑ Press (R) and the page requested will be shown.

11.4 Printing the output (.LIS) file

The .LIS file can be printed as SPSS/PC+ runs the command file, but is undesirable, for three reasons. First, it makes the whole process of running SPSS/PC+ very slow, as it keeps having to wait for the printer to catch up. Second, in its raw state the .LIS file contains a lot of material such as page headings that are not really wanted, so it is very extravagant on paper. Third, there are many occasions when the program fails because of some mistake in the command file, and it is wasteful to have a record of all these mistakes!

The easiest method of obtaining a printed copy of the .LIS file is to leave SPSS/PC+, return to DOS and then use the usual command:

`type a:fn.lis>prn (R)`

If the output file is called mine.lis, of course it is necessary to use that name instead of `fn.lis` in this command.

11.5 Editing the .LIS file

The original .LIS file contains a lot of unnecessary material such as page headings, messages about the time the task was completed and so on. If you intend to use the .LIS output from SPSS/PC+ in reports it is necessary to edit the .LIS file to get a clean version. (There are other ways of obtaining output in a form suitable for including in reports, considered in Chapter 22).

The simple way of obtaining a clean .LIS file is to word process it. Run your word processor in the usual way, and call up the .LIS file for editing. You can then remove unwanted sections, apply all the word processing facilities such as text styling and formatting, and print it out in the form you want. The word processing technique is probably the most convenient method for editing the .LIS file, especially as you are likely to be familiar with the conventions of your own word processor.

It is also possible to edit the .LIS file within SPSS/PC+. As explained above (Section 11.2), you can position the cursor in the top half of the screen where the .LIS file is shown, and use the *zoom* or *change size* facility to have this window fill the whole screen. Editing is done using the function keys. For example, deleting single lines or blocks of lines is accomplished using the F4 or F7 and F8 keys, as described in Section 8.4

There is a range of other editing functions which you can use: F5 accesses a *Search and Replace* facility so you can change any string of characters into a different one. This is achieved by pressing F5 and then selecting *fOrward change* or *bAckward change* from the minimenu.

So it is possible to edit the .LIS file within SPSS/PC+, and save the edited file using the F9 *Write whole file* route in the usual way. Note that if you have zoomed the .LIS file so it fills the whole screen, you will need to *unzoom* it by pressing Esc before F9 takes effect and allows you to save the file. When you press F9 (R), take the opportunity to type in a new name (such as a:clean2.LIS) for the file being saved, so there is no danger of losing it when SPSS/PC+ runs again. The edited file (clean2.lis) can then be printed when you have returned to DOS using the command:

```
type a:clean2.lis >prn (R)
```

The illustrations of SPSS/PC+ output (.LIS) files in this book have all been edited, using either the editing procedures within SPSS/PC+ or a word processor, to remove page headings and irrelevant items of information that are automatically included in the output. This is why the illustrations do not match exactly the full .LIS files produced by running the command files.

11.6 The .LOG file

The .LOG file created when SPSS/PC+ runs is stored on the hard disk (drive C), and is a list of the commands that SPSS/PC+ has carried out during the session. It can be inspected from DOS in the usual way if you are in the SPSS directory of drive C by typing

```
type SPSS.LOG (R)
```

From the root directory of drive C, type:

```
type \SPSS\SPSS.LOG (R)
```

The .LOG file from running excom2 is illustrated in Figure 11.1. It shows which page of the .LIS file contains the results of each command. It can be copied to the floppy disk, or printed out.

```
[Next command's output on page 1
TITLE 'SPSS Exercise 2'.
DATA LIST FILE 'a:exdat' FIXED / id 1-2 sex 4 employer 6 area 8 att1 10
    att2 12 att3 14 cust 16-18 sales 20-27 (2) dstd 29-30 dstm 31-32 dsty
    33-34 .
SET /LISTING 'a:ex2.lis'.
VARIABLE LABELS cust 'customers visited' dsty 'year started job'.
VALUE LABELS sex 1 'male' 2 'female' /area 1 'North' 2 'South'.
MISSING VALUE sex(3).
FREQUENCIES /VARIABLES sex area.
[Next command's output on page 5
FINISH.
```

Figure 11.1: The .LOG file produced when excom2 is run

12

The .SYS File

12.1 Uses and benefits of a .SYS file

Using the technique described so far, every time SPSS/PC+ is invoked, it has to go through the procedure of reading the data file, interpreting the layout of the data, obeying the instructions on missing values, variable labels and so on before it gets to the stage of doing the analysis. With large data files these preliminaries take some time, and it is frustrating to have to wait while the program deals with them before it gets round to doing one simple task that you forgot to ask for the last time. The way to abbreviate this is by creating a .SYS file.

A .SYS file is a special version of the data file, which incorporates the data description elements of the command file including VARIABLE NAMES and VALUE LABELS and the effects of some other commands such as RECODE which are explained later (Chapter 19). When you have created a .SYS file, you can tell SPSS/PC+ to read it and apply procedures to it, as though it were the original data file. But .SYS files are processed much faster than normal data files.

There is a second benefit from using .SYS files. If you have two sets of data and want to join them together into one set (as explained in Chapter 23), you have to use .SYS files to do it.

12.2 Creating a .SYS file

Find SAVE *by selecting* read or write data *from the main menu and moving right. Move cursor to* SAVE *in the submenu and press the right arrow key; the next submenu contains* /OUTFILE''.

To create a .SYS file, you write a command file that includes the data specifications (FILE LIST, VALUE LABELS and so on), and then add the line:

```
SAVE /OUTFILE 'A:fn.sys'.
```

using the actual filename instead of `fn` in this line.

The complete command file to create a .SYS file of the data in exdat is:

```
TITLE 'SPSS Exercise 2'.
DATA LIST FILE 'a:exdat' FIXED / id 1-2 sex 4 employer 6 area 8 att1 10
    att2 12 att3 14 cust 16-18 sales 20-27 (2) dstd 29-30 dstm 31-32 dsty
    33-34 .
VARIABLE LABELS cust 'customers visited' dsty 'year started job'.
VALUE LABELS sex 1 'male' 2 'female' /area 1 'North' 2 'South'.
MISSING VALUE sex(3).
SAVE /OUTFILE 'a:ex1.sys'.
```

When this command file is run, the .SYS file ex1.sys will be written on the floppy disk.

Exercise 12.1

Write the command file shown above to create a .SYS file of the exdat file. All except the last line are included in the command file excom2. Retrieve it and delete the SET /LISTING and FREQUENCIES lines. (In edit mode, use the F4 key and select *Delete* from the minimenu.) With the cursor on the MISSING VALUE line, move it to the end of that line, by pressing Ctrl right-arrow. Return to menu mode, and add the SAVE/OUTFILE 'a:ex1.sys' line. Save the file as syscom on the floppy disk, and run it. The file ex1.sys will be stored on the floppy.

12.3 Using the .SYS file

Find GET/FILE" *by selecting* read or write data *from main menu and pressing the right-arrow key. Move the cursor to* GET *in the submenu and press right-arrow key. The submenu contains* FILE".

Once the data has been stored in the form of a .SYS file, writing the command file for subsequent data analysis becomes much simpler. The .SYS file is retrieved with the GET command:

```
GET /FILE 'a:fn.sys'.
```

and procedures can then follow this line.

To use ex1.sys, use these commands:

```
GET /FILE 'A:ex1.SYS'·.
SET /LISTING 'a:sysout.lis'.
...Procedure lines....
```

(Remember that *SET/LISTING* is under *session control & info* in the main menu).

12.4 Modifying the .SYS file

There is one major drawback to .SYS files: they cannot be edited. They are stored in a particular format that can only be read by SPSS/PC+, and they cannot be brought into the scratchpad or listed on the screen. At first, this inability to edit a .SYS file may seem a major problem. If the data has a mistake in it, how can it be corrected? In fact, this is no problem at all. Remember the .SYS file was created by having the command file syscom (Exercise 12.1) read the original data file and then create the .SYS file with the SAVE /OUTFILE command. If you need to change the data, go back to the original data file (exdat) and edit that. Then retrieve the command file syscom, and run it again. It will save an outfile ex1.sys just as before, but this ex1.sys will be a version of the corrected data file.

Now that you are aware of .SYS files, you will probably use them almost all the time. (The remainder of this book uses ex1.sys rather than the original exdat file.) They are considerably more convenient than using the original data file, but of course the data and data definition commands must be correct before the .SYS file is created.

12.5 Viewing the contents of a .SYS file

To find SYSFILE INFO *from the Main menu, select* session control & info *and go right.*

As it is not possible to list .SYS files directly on the screen, it is easy to forget what each one contains. The technique for obtaining a summary of the contents of a .sys file is to use the SYSFILE INFO '' command: Paste it into the scratchpad, and type into the typing window the name of the .SYS file. When the command is run, using the usual F10 key, details of the file will be shown, including a list of the variables and the variable labels.

13

Getting the Results you want: Examining the Data

13.1 Introduction

Chapters 13-18 indicate the lines needed in the Command file to achieve certain statistical analyses, using the data in exdat to illustrate the various procedure commands. This chapter explains how to obtain outputs which allow you to check the system is reading the data file correctly and which provide an overall impression of the data.

As mentioned earlier, this is not a text on statistical analysis. It is assumed readers knows which statistics they want carried out, and what the statistics mean. A user who asks for a t-test, a Mann-Whitney or an analysis of variance presumably understands what these tests do and how to interpret the significance of a particular value of t, U, F and so on. So in this and the following chapters there is only a very brief statement of the use of each of the statistical procedures and how the output should be interpreted. In most instances, the printout obtained from SPSS/PC+ is straightforward. It may include additional material which you do not require and can ignore. You will find explanations in the manuals, if you are in difficulty, and the Appendix provides a recapitulation of statistical analysis which you may find useful.

If you have not yet done so, read Chapter 12 about the use of .SYS files. Since these are much easier to deal with, they will be used from now on. The first line of the Command files illustrating the various procedures is simply:

```
GET /FILE 'a:ex1.sys'.
```

This retrieves the data from exdat, together with the data description. If the procedure commands follow immediately after the GET /FILE instruction, the output will be sent to the file SPSS.LIS in the spss subdirectory on drive C. To have the output sent to another file (fn) on drive A, the first two lines of the command files needed to follow the examples shown in these chapters should be:

```
GET /FILE 'a:exl.sys'.
SET /LISTING 'a:fn'.
```

13.2 What does the data look like?

Before proceeding with detailed statistical investigation, it is worth having a rough overview of the data to reveal any peculiarities or possible errors in the data file. LIST and EXAMINE are two procedures which allow you to do this.

13.3 LIST

To find LIST *from the main Menu, select* analyze data, *go right, select* reports and tables, *and go right again.*

This procedure gives a simple listing of the data, and was mentioned in Chapter 10; an illustration of the output is given in Figure 10.1. Usually it is the first procedure, so that the data can be checked against the original records and you can ensure that the data file has an accurate copy of the figures. It is obviously pointless to proceed with further analysis until you are confident the data is encoded accurately and is being read correctly by the system. To obtain a listing of the data for all the variables in the data file, the command is:

```
LIST.
```

To have a list of a subset of the variables use:

```
LIST variable-name1 variable-name2.
```

So to obtain a listing of the values for the exdat variables `age` and `employer`, and send the output to ex.lis on the floppy disk, the commands are:

```
GET /FILE 'a:exl.sys'.
SET /LISTING 'a:ex.lis'.
LIST age employer.
```

To list the first n cases in the data file, use:

```
LIST /CASES n.
```

Remember to put a number instead of n in this command line.

LIST is particularly useful after a RECODE or a SORT procedure (described in Chapters 19 and 20), to confirm they have done what was intended.

13.4 EXAMINE

To find EXAMINE, *select* analyze data *from the main menu, go right, select* descriptive statistics *and go right again.*

```
      CUST
 Valid cases: 22.0   Missing cases: .0   Percent missing: .0

 Mean    50.818 Std Err     3.6269  Min    28.000  Skewness    .6051
 Median  44.500 Variance  289.3939  Max    83.000  S E Skew    .4910
 5%Trim  50.308 Std Dev    17.0116  Range  55.000  Kurtosis -1.0005
                                      IQR  30.000  S E Kurt    .9528
---------------------------------------------------------------------
      CUST
 Frequency    Stem &  Leaf

      1.00       2 .  8
      6.00       3 .  036899
      7.00       4 .  0123688
      1.00       5 .  8
      2.00       6 .  08
      4.00       7 .  1269
      1.00       8 .  3

 Stem width:    10
 Each leaf:        1 case(s)
---------------------------------------------------------------------
```

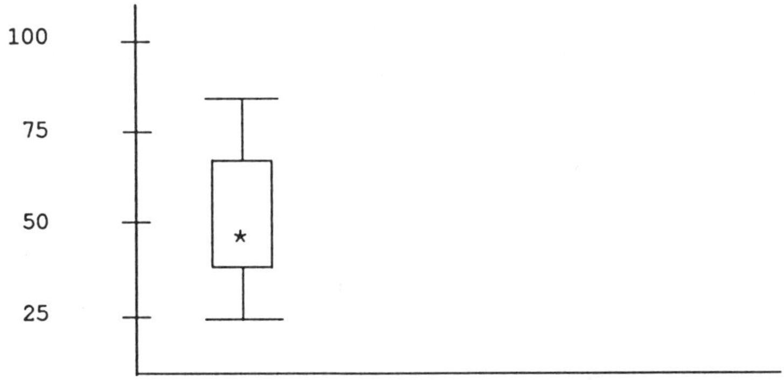


```
 Variables        CUST
 N of Cases         22.00
       Symbol Key:   *  - Median  (O) - Outlier  (E) - Extreme
---------------------------------------------------------------------
```

Figure 13.1: Output from the command EXAMINE /VARIABLES cust. Stem-leaf and boxplots are explained in Section 21.4

The EXAMINE procedure provides summary statistics (mean, standard deviation, range, minimum, maximum and so on) and graphical displays of data which will reveal impossible values (such as a mistaken coding of a value of 5 for sex in exdat), outlying values, unexpected gaps etc. It also gives a histogram of the data, stem-leaf plots, boxplots, and tests to see whether data is normally distributed.

The line for this procedure is:

```
EXAMINE /VARIABLES variable-name.
```

To have the procedure applied to the variable cust in exdat, the command lines are:

```
GET /FILE 'a:ex1.sys'.
SET /LISTING 'a:ex.lis'.
EXAMINE /VARIABLES cust.
```

This provides a listing of the summary statistics of the scores on the variable named, as shown in Figure 13.1. The printout shows a range of statistics including the mean, median, standard error, variance, standard deviation, minimum, maximum, range, interquartile range (IQR), and indices of skew. The figure for skewness indicates how non-symmetric the distribution is. A positive value on kurtosis indicates that the distribution of the scores has heavier tails than a normal distribution curve. The values for both skewness and kurtosis will be close to zero if the distribution is normally distributed. The stem-leaf plot and boxplot are explained in Section 21.4.

To get a list of the most extreme values of the variable, use:

```
EXAMINE /VARIABLES variable-name /STATISTICS ALL.
```

The printout then shows the five smallest and five largest values of the variable together with the case number of those scores. The case number is the number assigned to each case by the system when it reads the data file; the first case is number 1, the second number 2 and so on. The data file exdat includes ids, which are for this particular set of data the same as the case number, since they count up from 1 in regular sequence. But many data files do not do this: there may not be ids, or they may not be in sequence.

To obtain the EXAMINE statistics and plots for one variable according to the level of another variable, the command is:

```
EXAMINE /VARIABLES variable1 BY variable2.
```

So to examine the scores on cust for each employer, use:

```
EXAMINE /VARIABLES cust BY employer.
```

The printout shows the scores on cust for each employer. Part of the output from this command is shown in Figure 13.2. (The statistics for the complete set of scores on cust and the stem-leaf and boxplots have been deleted.)

```
       CUST
By  EMPLOYER  1

Valid cases:    8.0   Missing cases:   .0   Percent missing: .0

Mean      41.2500  Std Err     2.0420  Min   30.00  Skewness  -.8298
Median    41.5000  Variance   33.3571  Max   48.00  S E Skew   .7521
5% Trim   41.5000  Std Dev     5.7756  Range 18.00  Kurtosis  1.3531
                                       IQR    8.25  S E Kurt  1.4809
----------------------------------------------------------------


       CUST
By  EMPLOYER  2

Valid cases:    8.0   Missing cases:   .0   Percent missing: .0

Mean      44.0000  Std Err      5.1409  Min   28.00  Skewness  1.0903
Median    39.0000  Variance   211.4286  Max   71.00  S E Skew   .7521
5% Trim   43.3889  Std Dev     14.5406  Range 43.00  Kurtosis   .3348
                                        IQR   22.75  S E Kurt  1.4809
----------------------------------------------------------------


       CUST
By  EMPLOYER  3

Valid cases:    6.0   Missing cases:   .0   Percent missing: .0

Mean      72.6667  Std Err     3.6301  Min   58.00  Skewness  -.7947
Median    74.0000  Variance   79.0667  Max   83.00  S E Skew   .8452
5% Trim   72.9074  Std Dev     8.8919  Range 25.00  Kurtosis   .4550
                                       IQR   14.50  S E Kurt  1.7408
----------------------------------------------------------------
```

Figure 13.2: Extracts of output from the command EXAMINE /VARIABLES cust BY employer.

A frequency table is obtained with this command:

EXAMINE /VARIABLES variable-name /FREQUENCIES FROM (n) BY (b).

Put one number for n and another for b in this line, to get a table showing the frequency of responses in bands of size b starting at n. For example:

`EXAMINE /VARIABLES cust /FREQUENCIES FROM (20) BY (10).`

gives a table in which the values of the scores on the variable `cust` are grouped into bands starting at 20 and containing a range of 10. The centre of the bands are therefore 25, 35, 45 and so on and these are shown in the table (Figure 13.3) together with the frequency of scores in each band and the percentages.

CUST

Frequency Table

Bin Center	Freq	Pct	Valid Pct	Cum Pct
< 20				
25	1.00	4.55	4.55	4.55
35	6.00	27.27	27.27	31.82
45	7.00	31.82	31.82	63.64
55	1.00	4.55	4.55	68.18
65	2.00	9.09	9.09	77.27
75	4.00	18.18	18.18	95.45
85	1.00	4.55	4.55	100.00

Figure 13.3: Extract of output from the command EXAMINE /VARIABLES cust /FREQUENCIES FROM (20) BY (10).

To obtain a histogram, use:

`EXAMINE /VARIABLES variable-name /PLOT HISTOGRAM.`

which gives a histogram of the scores on the variable named. Histograms are explained further in Section 21.1.

13.5 A warning: Beware of means of nominal data

The procedures described above are used for the analysis of frequency data: how many respondents gave a particular answer or score on a particular variable. They also provide the mean and variability of the scores, as has been demonstrated. There is one point worth bearing in mind. SPSS/PC+ will happily give the mean of a discrete variable, and this may be meaningless. There are examples in the scientific literature of eminent researchers making this mistake and reporting that the mean score on sex was 1.5. With categorical data such as sex, where respondents are 1, 2 or 3 (representing sex unknown), the mean of the scores is literally nonsense. But

SPSS/PC+ does not know that; it only knows there is a set of figures, so it does not object when it is asked for the mean even if it is not appropriate to do so. It is the user's responsibility to look at the results of the analyses intelligently!

Exercise 13.1

Create the following command file, and save it as excom3:

```
GET /FILE 'a:ex1.sys'.
SET /LISTING 'a:ex3.lis'.
EXAMINE /VARIABLES cust.
EXAMINE /VARIABLES cust BY area /FREQUENCIES FROM (20) BY (10).
EXAMINE /VARIABLES area /PLOT HISTOGRAM.
```

Run this command file and examine the output to see the functions of the three EXAMINE lines. The output and comments on it are given in Appendix A.

14

Getting the Results you want: Frequency Data

14.1 How many respondents gave a particular answer? FREQUENCIES

To find the FREQUENCIES *command in the menus, select* analyze data, *go right, select* descriptive statistics, *go right again.* FREQUENCIES *is the first entry in the submenu that is then revealed. Go right again to reveal the lengthy submenu.*

Probably the first question you ask of your data is: how many people gave each alternative response to a particular question? The answer is obtained using the FREQUENCIES command:

```
FREQUENCIES /VARIABLES variable-name.
```

In exdat, for example, you may want to know how many respondents were from each employer, so the command file would be:

```
GET /FILE 'a:exl.sys'.
SET /LISTING 'a:fn'.
FREQUENCIES /VARIABLES employer.
```

The /VARIABLES section tells SPSS/PC+ which variables are to be analysed. An example of the FREQUENCIES procedure was included in excom2, and the output (stored in ex2.lis) is shown in Figure 10.3 in Chapter 10.

The program analyses a number of variables one after the other if they are listed like this:

`FREQUENCIES /VARIABLES variable1 variable2 variable3.`

The order of the variables does not have to match the order in the DATA LIST line. When using FREQUENCIES to analyse a number of variables specified one after the other in the DATA LIST line, there is a short form of referring to them. Rather than using:

`FREQUENCIES /VARIABLES sex employer area`

you can use:

`FREQUENCIES /VARIABLES sex TO area.`

This tells SPSS/PC+ to apply the frequencies command to all the variables listed successively in the DATA LIST line starting with `sex` and continuing as far as `area`.

In Figure 10.3, the labels for the different values of `sex` have been included in the table: the output indicates that 1 denotes male, 2 denotes female. This is the result of having put the VALUE LABELS command into the original command file, excom2.

In the tables obtained by FREQUENCIES, one can obtain some summary statistics: mean, standard deviation, maximum value and minimum value are shown, if one uses:

`FREQUENCIES /VARIABLES variable-name /STATISTICS.`

To obtain other statistics, select the /STATISTICS option from the submenu, and then specify which statistics are required from the list presented in the submenu. For example:

`FREQUENCIES /VARIABLES variable-name /STATISTICS ALL.`

gives additional statistics such as median, mode, variance, sum and measures of skew.

If some of the data is missing, in that some cases do not have data for the variable being analysed, or if one of the data values has been defined as indicating missing data using the MISSING VALUE command, the table shows the frequencies of these missing values. But these are not included in the calculation of percentages, nor in the calculation of summary statistics such as the mean.

The table presents the values of the variable in ascending order. For descending order, use the /FORMAT DVALUE command like this:

`FREQUENCIES /VARIABLES variable-name /FORMAT DVALUE.`

Alternatively, the table can give the most frequent values first if you use /FORMAT AFREQ. The least frequent values come first with /FORMAT DFREQ. These subcommands, DVALUE, AFREQ and DFREQ can be typed in: when /FORMAT has been pasted into the line, obtain a typing window with Alt T and type in the subcommand you want.

There may be occasions when you want the summary statistics but not the table. This is achieved using:

```
FREQUENCIES /VARIABLES variable-name /FORMAT NOTABLE/STATISTICS .
```

Histograms and barcharts of the responses can be obtained from the FREQUENCIES command; these are described in Section 21.1.

14.2 Obtaining summary statistics: DESCRIPTIVES

To find DESCRIPTIVES *command in the menus, select* analyze data, *go right, select* descriptive statistics, *go right again.* DESCRIPTIVES *is in the submenu that is then revealed. Go right again to see the submenu showing the alternatives available.*

This procedure provides summary statistics (such as mean and standard deviation) of scores on variables, but does not give median or mode. It does not provide the frequency table that the FREQUENCIES procedure provides. Particular statistics can be requested, but it is simpler to use ALL like this:

```
DESCRIPTIVES /VARIABLES variable-name /STATISTICS ALL.
```

Exercise 14.1

Create the following command file, and save it as excom4:

```
GET /FILE 'a:exl.sys'.
SET /LISTING 'a:ex4.lis'.
FREQUENCIES /VARIABLES sex employer.
FREQUENCIES /VARIABLES employer /FORMAT DVALUE.
FREQUENCIES /VARIABLES cust /FORMAT NOTABLE/STATISTICS ALL.
DESCRIPTIVES /VARIABLES cust /STATISTICS ALL.
```

Run this command file and examine the output to see the functions of the FREQUENCIES and DESCRIPTIVES procedures. The output is shown in Appendix A.

14.3 How is one variable related to another? Producing 2-dimensional tables: CROSSTABS

To find CROSSTABS *in the Menu, select* analyze data, *go right, select* descriptive statistics *and go right again. The submenu includes* CROSSTABS.

You often want to examine how scores on two (or more) variables are related; for example, in exdat, what is the relationship between sex and employer? This requires a two-dimensional table showing the number of people of each sex who are employed by each employer. Tables like this are obtained using CROSSTABS:

```
CROSSTABS /TABLES variable1 BY variable2.
```

To obtain the table of sex by employer for exdat, the line is:

```
GET /FILE 'a:ex1.sys'.
SET /LISTING 'a:ex.lis'.
CROSSTABS /TABLES sex BY employer.
```

This command line gives the table shown in Figure 14.1. The first-named variable (sex) forms the rows, and the second one forms the columns. (So the table can be turned round by reversing the order in which the variables are specified.) The figures in the cells of the table are the number of cases (e.g. in exdat, four males worked for employer 1). Row and columns totals are provided, and are also expressed as a percentage of the overall total of cases.

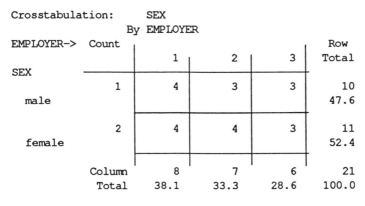

```
Crosstabulation:      SEX
                   By EMPLOYER
EMPLOYER->  Count                                    Row
                      1  |   2  |   3  |  Total
SEX         _____
            1      4      3      3         10
   male                                  47.6
            _____
            2      4      4      3         11
   female                                52.4
            _____
         Column    8      7      6         21
         Total   38.1   33.3   28.6    100.0
```

Number of Missing Observations =   1

Figure 14.1: Output from the command CROSSTABS /TABLES sex BY employer.

Note that in Figure 14.1, the total is 21 and one missing observation is shown; this is because the original data had one case where `sex` was coded as 3, indicating the sex of that respondent was unknown. Consequently there are only 21 cases that can be used in the `sex` by `employer` table.

You may want a further breakdown of the figures, with separate tables of `variable1` by `variable2` for each level of `variable3`; for example, suppose we want a sex by employer table, like that shown in Figure 14.1 but for each area group separately. This is achieved by:

`CROSSTABS /TABLES variable1 BY variable2 BY variable3.`

For example:

`CROSSTABS /TABLES sex BY employer BY area.`

`Area` here is referred to as a control variable, and you can have up to eight of them (so the line contains the word BY nine times!)

It is often helpful to have the frequencies expressed as percentages as well as the actual frequencies themselves. To have the frequencies as percentages of the total number of cases included in the table, use /OPTIONS 5 as in this line:

`CROSSTABS /TABLES employer BY sex /OPTIONS 5.`

If /OPTIONS 18 is used, the table (Figure 14.2) shows the actual frequency of cases in each cell, the expected value if there were no relationship between the two variables tabulated, the frequencies as a percentage of the total in the row, as a percentage of the total in the column, and as percentage of the overall total. There are also figures for residual, std res and adj res which are associated with the chi-square test and are unlikely to be needed. (The residual is the difference between the observed and expected values.)

14.4 Chi-square

To apply the chi-square test, it is necessary to use CROSSTABS /STATISTICS 1. *To find* CROSSTABS *in the Menu, select* analyze data, *go right, select* descriptive statistics *and go right again. The submenu includes* CROSSTABS. *Go right again for a submenu including* /TABLES *and* /STATISTICS.

The chi-square test is used with nominal data, where respondents have been allocated to categories (e.g. sex, area). The test compares the number of cases falling into each cell of the table with the frequency that would be expected if there were no association between the two variables that form the table.

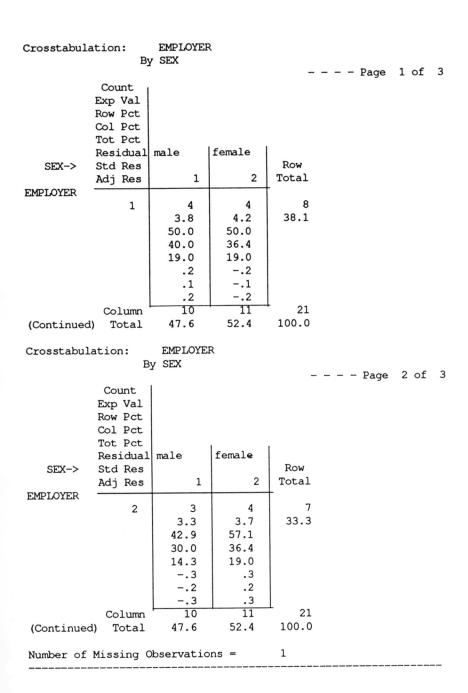

Figure 14.2: Extract of output from the command CROSSTABS /TABLES employer BY sex /OPTIONS 18. Note: The table for employer 3 has been deleted.

To obtain a chi-square test, use the CROSSTABS procedure with the /STATISTICS 1 option:

```
CROSSTABS /TABLES variable1 BY variable2 /STATISTICS 1.
```

The STATISTICS 1 does the chi-square test or the Fisher exact test if that is needed by the data in a 2 x 2 table.

Figure 14.3 shows the output from these commands:

```
GET /FILE 'a:ex1.sys'.
SET /LISTING 'a:ex.lis'.
CROSSTABS /TABLES sex BY area /STATISTICS 1.
```

The frequency table, showing the number of cases in each cell of the table, is followed by the value of chi-square, the degrees of freedom *(D.F.)*, and the probability *(Significance)*. (The concept of statistical significance and the principles of the chi-square test are summarised in the Appendix.) If the Significance value is equal to or less than .05, you can conclude that the chi-square test indicates that there is a significant association between the two variables.

The chi-square test is only valid if the expected frequencies for the cells in the table are sufficiently large: no cell should have an expected frequency less than 1 and fewer than 20% of the cells should have an expected frequency of less than 5. Below the table, the printout indicates the smallest expected frequency *(Min E.F.)* and the number of cells with an expected frequency of less than 5 *(Cells with E.F.<5)*. These figures indicate whether the chi-square test can validly be used on the data in the table.

With 2 x 2 tables, a different formula for chi-square is used which incorporates a correction for continuity. Figure 14.3 shows the chi-square values with and without this correction: the first of the two values is the one to use. If N is less than 20 in a 2 x 2 table, the Fisher Exact test should be used, rather than chi-square: SPSS/PC+ will do this for you automatically if it is needed.

If the test is not valid, you must either alter the data table, amalgamating categories to remove cells with small expected frequencies, and re-analyse the data. or collect more data. Figure 14.3 shows that the chi-square test is not valid on this table, as more than 20% of cells have an expected frequency smaller than 5; since it would not be meaningful to amalgamate groups, it would be necessary to collect more data in order to test the hypothesis that there is a tendency for sex to be related to area of the country in which people work.

```
Crosstabulation:      SEX
                   By AREA
```

```
           Count   North    South
   AREA->                             Row
                        1        2  Total
SEX
                1       3        7      10
       male                         47.6
                2       6        5      11
      female                        52.4
           Column      9       12      21
            Total    42.9     57.1   100.0
```

```
Chi-Square    D.F.   Significance   Min E.F.  Cells with E.F.< 5
----------    ----   ------------   --------  ------------------
  .48125       1        .4879         4.286     2 of 4 ( 50.0%)
 1.28864       1        .2563              ( Before Yates Correction )
```

```
Number of Missing Observations =     1
```

Figure 14.3: Output from the command CROSSTABS /TABLES sex BY area /STATISTICS 1.

Exercise 14.2

Create the following command file, and save it as excom5:

```
GET /FILE 'a:ex1.sys'.
SET /LISTING 'a:ex5.lis'.
CROSSTABS /TABLES area BY employer /OPTIONS 5.
CROSSTABS /TABLES sex BY employer /STATISTICS 1.
CROSSTABS /TABLES sex BY employer BY area.
```

Run this command file and examine the output to see what these CROSSTABS lines achieve. The output is illustrated in Appendix A.

15

Getting the Results you want: Measures of Central Tendency and Dispersion

15.1 Totals, means and standard deviations

To obtain the mean and standard deviation of scores on a variable, use one of the following:

```
EXAMINE /VARIABLES variable-name.
FREQUENCIES /VARIABLES variable-name /STATISTICS ALL.
DESCRIPTIVES /VARIABLES variable-name /STATISTICS ALL.
```

The total of a set of scores is given by the FREQUENCIES and DESCRIPTIVES comands, but not by EXAMINE.

EXAMINE is covered in Section 13.4, FREQUENCIES and DESCRIPTIVES in Sections 14.1 and 14.2.

Note that when carrying out parametric statistical tests, such as the t-test, the output will give the means and variances of the data, so there is no need to obtain them using a separate procedure.

To obtain a barchart or histogram (explained in Section 21.1) use:

```
FREQUENCIES /VARIABLES variable-name /BARCHART.
FREQUENCIES /VARIABLES variable-name /HISTOGRAM.
```

15.2 Medians

To find the median of a set of scores, use the FREQUENCIES procedure:

```
FREQUENCIES /VARIABLES variable-name /STATISTICS ALL.
```

This command file would give the median score on `sales` in exdat:

```
GET /FILE 'a:exl.sys'.
SET /LISTING 'a:ex.lis'.
FREQUENCIES /VARIABLES sales /STATISTICS ALL.
```

15.3 Finding the means and standard deviations of subgroups of the respondents: MEANS

To find MEANS, *select* analyze data, *go right, select* descriptive statistics *and go right again. The submenu revealed includes* MEANS *as one entry.*

We frequently want to know the scores of subgroups from the data; for example, in exdat, assume we want the mean scores on `sales` for males and females. There are a number of ways of obtaining this information, but one of the easiest is to use the MEANS procedure. The general form of the command is:

```
MEANS /TABLES variable1 BY variable2.
```

For example, the output shown in Figure 15.1 shows the mean sales for each of the two sex groups. It was produced by these commands:

```
Summaries of    SALES
By levels of    SEX

Variable        Value  Label            Mean     Std Dev   Cases

For Entire Population              5831.9205  2377.9699      21

SEX                1  male          5950.6370  2772.4555      10
SEX                2  female        5723.9964  2089.1906      11

    Total Cases =      22
Missing Cases =       1 OR    4.5 PCT.
----------------------------------------------------------------
```

Figure 15.1: Output from the command MEANS /TABLES sales BY sex

```
GET /FILE 'a:ex1.sys'.
SET /LISTING 'a:ex.lis'.
MEANS /TABLES sales BY sex.
```

Observe that the respondent whose sex is unknown, who was given a sex score of 3 (missing value) is not included in the table, and is shown as the missing case at the end of the printout.

If you wanted the mean scores on sales for the separate sex groups and then for the separate area groups, the command would be:

```
MEANS /TABLES sales BY sex area.
```

To have the output show the sum of scores for each group, use OPTIONS 6, and to obtain the variances OPTIONS 12:

```
MEANS /TABLES sales BY sex /OPTIONS 6 8 12.
```

There is often a problem here, and the program will stop, complaining that the table is too wide. Overcome this by including 8 in the /OPTIONS list as shown above. (It needs to be typed in, as it is not included in the /OPTIONS submenu unless you are using Extended menus.) It has the effect of suppressing the printing of the value labels, and so makes the table narrower.

Exercise 15.1

Create the following command file, and save it as excom6:

```
GET /FILE 'a:ex1.sys'.
SET /LISTING 'a:ex6.lis'.
MEANS /TABLES sales BY sex area.
MEANS /TABLES sales BY sex/ OPTIONS 6 8 12.
```

Run this command file and examine the output to see how to obtain the means of subgroups of cases. The results are shown in Appendix A.

16

Getting the Results you want: Parametric Statistical Tests

16.1 Introduction

This chapter describes the commands needed to obtain the more common parametric statistical tests. These are used to compare sets of scores when you can make certain assumptions about the data. These assumptions are given in the Appendix, section A7: you have to be able to assume the data has been measured on an interval scale (rather than a nominal or rank scale), is normally distributed, and the subgroups of data have equal variance. If these assumptions cannot be made, you should use non-parametric analyses, which are covered in Chapter 18.

Note that the examples shown here use the names of the variables in the exdat file; if you are applying the commands to a set of data with different variable names, you must of course use those variable names.

16.2 One-way analysis of variance

To find MEANS, *select* analyze data, *go right, select* descriptive statistics *and go right again. The submenu revealed includes* MEANS *as one entry.*

To find ONEWAY *in the menu, select* analyze data, *go right, select* comparing group means *and go right again.*

One-way analysis of variance is used to compare the mean scores of three or more groups of respondents on a particular variable. It involves calculating the F-ratio, the ratio of the variance arising from the difference between the groups to the variance arising within the groups. The one-way analysis of variance can be obtained using either of these commands:

```
MEANS /TABLES variable1 BY variable2 /STATISTICS 1.
ONEWAY /VARIABLES variable1 BY variable2(a,b).
```

ONEWAY allows you to compare pairs of sets of scores, with the range tests, and is probably the more useful procedure. When using ONEWAY, after BY you must state the independent variable and specify its maximum and minimum values in the brackets.

To compare the mean score on the variable cust (number of customers visited) of the respondents from each of the three employers in the exdat file, the relevant command file is either of the following:

```
GET /FILE 'a:ex1.sys'.
SET /LISTING 'a:ex.lis'.
MEANS /TABLES cust BY employer /STATISTICS 1.

GET /FILE 'a:ex1.sys'.
SET /LISTING 'a:ex.lis'.
ONEWAY /VARIABLES cust BY employer(1,3).
```

With ONEWAY, to obtain the mean, standard deviation and other summary statistics of each group being compared, you need to use the /STATISTICS subcommand:

```
ONEWAY /VARIABLES variable1 BY variable2(a,b) /STATISTICS 1.
```

Figure 16.1 illustrates the result of this subcommand. Tests of homogeneity of variance are provided if you use /STATISTICS 3. The two requests can be combined with:

```
ONEWAY /VARIABLES variable1 BY variable2(a,b) /STATISTICS 1 3.
```

The first section of Figure 16.1 is the usual analysis of variance table, showing the degrees of freedom, sum of squares, mean square between groups and within groups. The F ratio is the between groups mean square divided by the within groups mean square. The probability associated with F is given in the final column: if it is less than 0.05, this shows there is a significant difference between the groups being compared.

The second section of Figure 16.1 was produced by incorporating /STATISTICS 1 in the procedure command. It provides summary statistics for the groups being compared; as can be seen, the mean for group 1 (those respondents employed by employer 1) is 41.25, the standard deviation is 5.7756, the standard error is 2.0420. The 95% confidence limits for the mean are followed by the minimum and maximum scores on cust for this group of respondents. (Standard error and confidence limits are explained in the Appendix section A4.)

```
- - - - - - - - O N E W A Y - - - - - - - - - -
     Variable  CUST
By Variable  EMPLOYER
                          Analysis of Variance
                          Sum of        Mean          F
Source              D.F.  Squares       Squares     Ratio  Prob.
Between Groups        2   3968.4394    1984.2197   17.8773  .0000
Within Groups        19   2108.8333     110.9912
Total                21   6077.2727
```

```
- - - - - - - - - O N E W A Y - - - - - - - - - -
                   Standard   Standard
Group   Count  Mean  Deviation  Error   95 Pct Conf Int for Mean
Grp 1      8  41.2500   5.7756  2.0420   36.4215  To  46.0785
Grp 2      8  44.0000  14.5406  5.1409   31.8438  To  56.1562
Grp 3      6  72.6667   8.8919  3.6301   63.3353  To  81.9980
Total     22  50.8182  17.0116  3.6269   43.2757  To  58.3607

Group      Minimum      Maximum
Grp 1      30.0000      48.0000
Grp 2      28.0000      71.0000
Grp 3      58.0000      83.0000
Total      28.0000      83.0000
```

```
- - - - - - - - - - O N E W A Y - - - - - - - - - - -
     Variable  CUST
  By Variable  EMPLOYER

Multiple Range Test
Scheffe Procedure
Ranges for the   .050 level -
        3.75    3.75
The ranges above are table ranges.
The value actually compared with Mean(J)-Mean(I) is..
        7.4495 * Range * Sqrt(1/N(I) + 1/N(J))

(*) Denotes pairs of groups significantly different at the   .050
level
```

```
- - - - - - - - - O N E W A Y - - - - - - - - - - -
     Variable  CUST
     (Continued)
                         G G G
                         r r r
                         p p p
     Mean       Group    1 2 3
     41.2500    Grp 1
     44.0000    Grp 2
     72.6667    Grp 3    * *
```

Figure 16.1: Output from the command ONEWAY /VARIABLES cust BY
employer(1,3) /RANGES SCHEFFE /STATISTICS 1.

If the one-way analysis of variance shows that there is a significant difference between the three (or more) groups, it does not specify where this difference lies. For example, the results of the analysis of variance on the cust scores shows there is a difference between the employers in terms of how many customers were visited (Figure 16.1 shows F=17.8773; p=0.0000 indicates the F value is highly significant). But is there a significant difference between employers 1 and 2, between 1 and 3, between 2 and 3? These questions are answered using Scheffe, Duncan or Tukey tests, which can be requested in the ONEWAY command with the subcommand /RANGES as in these examples:

```
ONEWAY /VARIABLES cust BY employer(1,3) /RANGES SCHEFFE.
ONEWAY /VARIABLES cust BY employer(1,3) /RANGES DUNCAN.
ONEWAY /VARIABLES cust BY employer(1,3) /RANGES TUKEY.
```

The output from ONEWAY with /RANGES SCHEFFE is illustrated in Figure 16.1. The cust scores in exdat were subjected to an analysis of variance, summary statistics were requested, and the Scheffe test conducted with these commands:

```
GET /FILE 'a:ex1.sys'.
SET /LISTING 'a:ex.lis'.
ONEWAY /VARIABLES cust BY employer(1,3) /RANGES SCHEFFE /STATISTICS 1.
```

The final section of the output indicates, with the asterisks, that group 3 (i.e. employer 3) is significantly different from both group 1 and group 2. The absence of asterisks shows that groups 1 and 2 do not differ from each other.

16.3 Within-subjects t-test

To find T-TEST *in the menu, select* analyze data, *go right, select* comparing group means *and go right again.*

The t-test is used to compare two sets of scores. When comparing the scores of the same respondents on two variables, you need the within-subjects (paired) t-test. The paired t-test would be used, for example, to compare the scores of the respondents in exdat on att1 and att2, to discover whether the mean response to att1 was different from the mean response to att2.

The general form of the command for a within-subjects t-test is:

```
T-TEST /PAIRS variable1 variable2.
```

where the two variables named are the ones to be compared.

You can obtain a set of t-tests by naming more variables after the /PAIRS subcommand. To have t-tests comparing variable1 and variable2, variable2 and variable3, variable1 and variable3, use:

```
T-TEST /PAIRS variable1 variable2 variable3.
```

Figure 16.2 shows the output from the command:

```
T-TEST /PAIRS att1 att2.
```

After the means, standard deviations and standard errors of the scores on each variable, it provides the mean of the difference scores, the correlation between the two sets of scores and the significance (probability) of the correlation, the t-value, degrees of freedom and the two-tailed probability of that t-value having arisen by chance. Note that if the probability level is .0000, this indicates the value is highly significant: the probability is less than .0001. Figure 16.2 shows that there is a significant difference between the scores on att1 and att2, as the probability level is less than .05.

```
Paired samples t-test:   ATT1
                         ATT2

Variable      Number              Standard    Standard
             of Cases    Mean     Deviation     Error

ATT1            22       2.5455     1.101        .235
ATT2            22       3.0909      .921        .196

(Difference) Standard Standard | 2-Tail    | t    Degrees of  2-Tail
   Mean     Deviation  Error   | Corr Prob |Value  Freedom     Prob.

  -.5455      .800     .171     |.700  .000 | 3.20    21        .004
```

Figure 16.2: Output from the command T-TEST /PAIRS att1 att2.

16.4 Between-subjects t-test

To find T-TEST *in the menu, select* analyze data, *go right, select* comparing group means *and go right again.*

To compare the scores of two groups of different subjects on one variable, it is necessary to use the between-subjects t-test. For example, to compare the sales figures of the males and females in exdat you require a between-subjects t-test. The general form of the command is:

```
T-TEST /GROUPS variable1(x,y) /VARIABLES variable2.
```

After /GROUPS, you must specify the variable used to identify the two groups to be compared, and state the value of the groups' codes on this variable. The variable named after /VARIABLE specifies the scores which are t-tested.

Using the data in exdat, the line below compares the scores on `sales` of the groups from employers 1 and 3:

`T-TEST /GROUPS employer(1,3) /VARIABLES sales.`

The output from this command is shown in Figure 16.3. Below the summary statistics for each group, it gives an F value and two alternative values of t. If the probability associated with F is less than .05, use the t value for the separate variance estimate, otherwise the t value for the pooled variance estimate is the one to take. Figure 16.3 indicates that there is a significant difference between the sales of respondents from employers 1 and 3, as the probability value is less than .05. Observe that the table defines the two employers as group 1 and group 2, but the top of the output states that group 1 is employer 1 and group 2 is employer 3.

```
Independent samples of  EMPLOYER

Group 1:  EMPLOYER  EQ 1          Group 2:  EMPLOYER  EQ 3

t-test for:  SALES
                      Number                Standard     Standard
                     of Cases     Mean      Deviation     Error

          Group 1       8      5333.2313    2761.360     976.288
          Group 2       6      8207.4150     925.178     377.702
```

		Pooled Variance Estimate			Separate Variance Estimate		
F	2-Tail	t	Degrees of	2-Tail	t	Degrees of	2-Tail
Value	Prob.	Value	Freedom	Prob.	Value	Freedom	Prob.
8.91	.028	-2.43	12	.032	-2.75	8.97	.023

Figure 16.3: Output from the command T-TEST /GROUPS employer(1,3)/ VARIABLES sales.

Exercise 16.1

Create the following command file, and save it as excom7:

```
GET /FILE 'a:ex1.sys'.
SET /LISTING 'a:ex7.lis'.
T-TEST /PAIRS att1 att3.
T-TEST /GROUPS employer(1,2) /VARIABLES sales.
```

Run this command file to compare the respondents' scores on att1 and att3, and to compare the sales data for employers 1 and 2. The output is similar to Figures 16.2 and 16.3.

16.5 Two-way analysis of variance

To find ANOVA *in the menu, select* analyze data, *go right, select* comparing group means *and go right again.*

A two-way analysis of variance is used to compare the scores of respondents who can be divided according to two independent variables. For example, in exdat we have scores on sales for respondents who are divided by sex and divided by area. Both these are between-subjects factors, since any one person is either male or female and works either in the North or in the South. Suppose we want to compare the sales scores of males and females, and of those working in the North with those working in the South, and also want to see whether there is an interaction between sex and area. (For example, do men do better on sales than women when they working in the North but not when they are working in the South?) This analysis is obtained using the ANOVA procedure.

Note that ANOVA is only applicable when both the independent variables are between-subjects. This means that on each variable taken separately any individual respondent can only be in one of the groups. For example, sex is a between-subjects variable since any individual must be one or the other, and cannot be both.

To do a two-way ANOVA with two independent variables that are between-subjects factors, the command is:

```
ANOVA /VARIABLES dependent_ve BY indep_ve1(min,max) indep_ve2(min,max).
```

So the two-way analysis of variance comparing sales of males and females and of different geographical areas, is obtained with this command file:

```
GET /FILE 'a:ex.sys'.
SET /LISTING 'a:ex.lis'.
ANOVA /VARIABLES sales BY area(1,2) sex(1,2) /STATISTICS 3.
```

The /STATISTICS 3 gives the cell means for the dependent variable.

```
                    * * *  C E L L   M E A N S  * * *
              SALES
          BY  AREA
              SEX

TOTAL POPULATION
   5831.92
 (     21)


AREA
        1             2
   6158.48    5587.00
 (     9)  (     12)


SEX
        1             2
   5950.64    5724.00
 (    10)  (     11)


              SEX
                1           2
AREA     1   5321.34   6577.05
           (     3)  (     6)

         2   6220.33   4700.33
           (     7)  (     5)

          * * *  A N A L Y S I S   O F   V A R I A N C E  * * *
                   SALES
              BY   AREA
                   SEX
```

Source of Variation	Sum of Squares	DF	Mean Square	F	Signif of F
Main Effects	2430917.664	2	1215458.832	.204	.818
AREA	2161857.779	1	2161857.779	.362	.555
SEX	751285.695	1	751285.695	.126	.727
2-way Interactions	9141051.914	1	9141051.914	1.531	.233
AREA SEX	9141051.914	1	9141051.914	1.531	.233
Explained	11571969.578	3	3857323.193	.646	.596
Residual	101522846.164	17	5971932.127		
Total	113094815.742	20	5654740.787		

```
       22 Cases were processed.
        1 Cases (  4.5 PCT) were missing.
```

Figure 16.4: Output from the command ANOVA /VARIABLES sales BY area(1,2) sex(1,2) /STATISTICS 3.

The output from this command is shown in Figure 16.4. The first part is the cell means, produced as a result of including the /STATISTICS 3 subcommand. It shows the overall mean score on `sales`, the means for each category of `area`, for each category of `sex` and for each `area`/`sex` group. The numbers in brackets show the number of respondents upon which each mean is based. The analysis of variance table is then given; in this instance, none of the factors is significant as can be seen from the final column of Significance values of F: they are all larger than .05. The one case missing is the respondent from the original data file who had not indicated their sex, and was scored 3 (the missing value) on that variable.

17

Getting the Results you want: Correlation

17.1 Parametric (Pearson) correlation

To find CORRELATIONS *in the menu, select* analyze data, *go right, select* correlation & regression *and go right.*

To find the parametric correlation between two variables, use the command:

CORRELATIONS /VARIABLES variable1 variable2 /STATISTICS 1.

The /STATISTICS 1 tells SPSS/PC+ to print out the mean and standard deviation of the variables being correlated. It can be omitted.

```
Variable        Cases          Mean          Std Dev

ATT1             22           2.5455          1.1010
ATT2             22           3.0909           .921

Correlations:  ATT1          ATT2

   ATT1        1.0000         .7001**
   ATT2         .7001**      1.0000

N of cases:    22            1-tailed Signif:  * - .01  ** - .001

" . " is printed if a coefficient cannot be computed
```

Figure 17.1: Output from the command CORRELATIONS /VARIABLES att1 att2 /STATISTICS 1.

To obtain all the correlations between three variables, list the variables like this:

```
CORRELATIONS /VARIABLES variable1 variable2 variable3.
```

The correlation between responses on `att1` and `att2` in exdat, shown in Figure 17.1, was found with:

```
GET /FILE 'a:ex1.sys'.
SET /LISTING 'a:ex.lis'.
CORRELATIONS /VARIABLES att1 att2 /STATISTICS 1.
```

The output gives the correlation and indicates, by asterisks, its significance level.

17.2 Scattergrams

To find PLOT *in the menu, select* graph data *from the main menu and go right.*

There are a number of ways of obtaining a scattergram, as described in Sections 21.2 and 21.3. One method is to use:

```
PLOT /PLOT variable1 WITH variable2.
```

which produces a scattergram but does not yield the correlation coefficient.

The easiest procedure for obtaining both the correlation and the scattergram is to use:

```
PLOT /FORMAT REGRESSION /PLOT variable1 WITH variable2.
```

As an illustration, Figure 17.2 shows the output from:

```
PLOT /FORMAT REGRESSION /PLOT att1 WITH att2.
```

The scatterplot is given, followed by the correlation, and statistics on the regression line (slope, intercept etc). The figures in the scatterplot indicate the number of cases occurring at that intersection of values on the two variables plotted.

The best-fitting straight line through the data points is obtained if one draws a line connecting the R characters on the left and right vertical axes.

Exercise 17.1

Create the following command file, and save it as excom8:

```
GET /FILE 'a:ex1.sys'.
SET /LISTING 'a:ex8.lis'.
CORRELATIONS /VARIABLES cust sales /STATISTICS 1.
PLOT /TITLE 'Customer visit against sales'
   /PLOT cust WITH sales.
```

Run this command file and examine the output. The CORRELATIONS command gives a table similar to Figure 17.1. The PLOT command produces a scatterplot similar to Figure 17.2, but without the correlation statistics since the subcommand /FORMAT REGRESSION is not included.

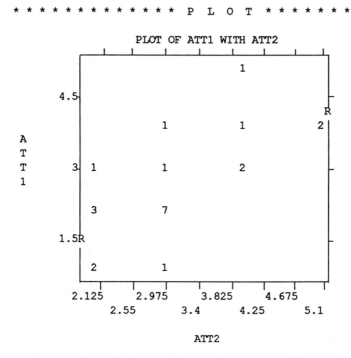

```
* * * * * * * * * * * * *  P  L  O  T  * * * * * * * * * * * * * *

                    PLOT OF ATT1 WITH ATT2

                                      1

        4.5                                              R
                                                         2
   A             1              1              2
   T
   T         3  1              1              2
   1
                 3              7

        1.5R

                 2              1

            2.125        2.975        3.825        4.675
                  2.55          3.4          4.25          5.1

                            ATT2
```

22 cases plotted. Regression statistics of ATT1 on ATT2:
Correlation   .70006 R Squared .49009 SE of Est .80559 Sig .0003
Intercept(SE) −.04082(.61438)   Slope(SE)   .83673(.19085)

Figure 17.2: Output from the command PLOT /FORMAT REGRESSION /PLOT att1 WITH att2.

17.3 Multiple Regression

To find REGRESSION in the menu, select analyze data, *go right, select* correlation & regression *and go right. REGRESSION is in the submenu.*

Multiple regression is a procedure in which you predict the score on a dependent variable from the scores on a number of independent variables (see Appendix Section A10.5). In exdat, we have the data on each person's sales. We can readily correlate the sales score with the scores on the other variables, such as number of customers visited, response to the att1 question and so on. The correlation between sales and customers visited is 0.7266 (Exercise 17.1). The regression equation, which expresses the relationship between sales and cust as an equation can be obtained using the REGRESSION command like this:

`REGRESSION /VARIABLES sales cust /DEPENDENT sales /METHOD ENTER.`

In this procedure, you must name the variables, specify the one that is the dependent variable, and also specify the method to be used. In this simple example, with just one independent variable (cust), the subcommand shown above is sufficient.

In multiple regression, you use a number of independent variables to predict the dependent variable. For example, you can predict sales from cust (number of customers visited), since the correlation between these two variables is 0.7266, significant at the .001 level. But will the prediction be better if you also consider the person's response to the att1 and att2 questions? It is with this type of problem that multiple regression is concerned.

The techniques of multiple regression are more advanced than most beginners with SPSS/PC+ are likely to need. Consequently, the topic is not pursued here, other than demonstrating a comparatively simple example:

`REGRESSION /VARIABLES sales cust att1 att2 att3 /DEPENDENT sales /METHOD ENTER.`

This asks for multiple regression of sales, with the four variables cust, att1, att2, and att3 being usesd as independent (predictor) variables. The output from this command is given in Figure 17.3.

It shows the dependent variables is sales, and that the multiple regression method used was the one known as 'enter'. After listing the predictor variables that were entered into the equation, it gives the Multiple R (.73362 in Fig 17.3) which is the correlation between the predictor variables combined and the dependent variable. R squared indicates the proportion of the variability in the dependent variable which is accounted for by the multiple regression equation. The figure labelled '*Adjusted R square*' is an estimate of R squared for the population (rather than the sample from which the data was obtained), and includes a correction for shrinkage.

The analysis of variance table shown in Fig 17.3 shows the sum of squares explained by the regression equation and the 'residual' sum of squares. The residual sum of squares is the variability in the dependent variable which is left unexplained by the regression equation. The F statistic is obtained by dividing the Mean Square regression by the Mean Square residual. If F is significant (the probability value shown is less than 0.05), one can assume there is a linear relationship between the predictor and the dependent variables and that the regression equation allows you to predict the dependent variable at greater than chance level.

```
    * * * *   M U L T I P L E    R E G R E S S I O N   * * * *
Listwise Deletion of Missing Data
Equation Number 1     Dependent Variable..    SALES
Beginning Block Number  1.  Method:  Enter


Equation Number 1     Dependent Variable..    SALES


Variable(s) Entered on Step Number
    1..    CUST
    2..    ATT3
    3..    ATT2
    4..    ATT1


Multiple R             .73362
R Square               .53820
Adjusted R Square      .42954
Standard Error    1755.50691


Analysis of Variance
                      DF      Sum of Squares        Mean Square
Regression             4      61058696.52776     15264674.13194
Residual              17      52390676.44811      3081804.49695


F =       4.95316        Signif F =   .0078
--------------------------------------------------------------------
Equation Number 1     Dependent Variable..    SALES


------------------- Variables in the Equation --------------------
Variable            B          SE B        Beta          T   Sig T

CUST            94.08951     26.41230      .68864      3.562  .0024
ATT3           214.41919    521.54581      .10900       .411  .6861
ATT2          -186.74295    664.80260     -.07401      -.281  .7822
ATT1           188.65193    594.57453      .08936       .317  .7549
(Constant)     444.19126   4131.18896                   .108  .9156


End Block Number   1   All requested variables entered.
--------------------------------------------------------------------
```

*Figure 17.3: Output from the command REGRESSION /VARIABLES sales cust att1
att2 att3/DEPENDENT sales /METHOD ENTER.*

The final part of Fig 17.3 lists the predictor variables and some statistics associated with each one. B is the regression coefficient for the variable. In the present example, we have a regression equation like this:

sales = w1(cust) + w2(att3) + w3(att2) + w4(att1)

The values of w1, w2 etc are regression coefficients and determine how much weight is given to each of the predictor variables; the last section of Fig 17.3 shows the regression coefficients (B) for each predictor variable. It is important to realise that these B values do not show how important each predictor variable is; the relative importance is shown when the B values have been transformed into standard scores, when they are referred to as beta. These are given in Fig 17.3, and indicate that cust has much more influence on the dependent variable, sales, than do att1, att2 or att3.

The final columns of this part of the output show T values and their probabilities *(Sig T)*. These indicate whether the regression coefficients for each variable are greater than zero. In Fig 17.3, the T values for att1, att2 and att3 are not significant, so one would conclude that these variables do not predict sales. The T value for cust is significant ($p = .0024$), so this does predict sales.

The final row of the table, labelled *(constant),* refers to the intercept of the regression line. The T value indicates whether it is significantly different from zero.

A full explanation of the numerous regression procedure subcommands will be found in the SPSS/PC+ manual.

17.4 Rank Correlation

The technique for obtaining a rank correlation is described in Section 18.9

18

Getting the Results you want: Non-parametric Analysis

18.1 Non-parametric tests

To find the non-parametric analyses, select analyze data *from the main menu, go right and select* other *from the submenu; go right again and select* NPAR *from the submenu. Go right: the submenu allows you to select the non-parametric test you want.*

Non-parametric tests are used when the data does not lend itself to parametric statistical analysis, because it is rank data, or is skewed, or the groups show unequal variance. A wide range of non-parametric tests is available in the NPAR command. In this chapter only the more commonly used ones are considered, but others will be found in the same menu as those described here. A description of these tests will be found in the Appendix (A8 and A9).

18.2 Chi-square for two or more independent samples

This chi-square is not located in the NPAR *section, but is found under* FREQUENCIES.

If the data is nominal, and the numbers act merely as labels for the various conditions (as when 1 is used to denote male and 2 to denote female), the analysis will depend on frequency counts, tables of cross-tabulations, chi-square. The method for obtaining chi-square for two or more samples was covered in Section 14.4; just to recapitulate, to obtain a chi-square on the data for variable1 (e.g. `sex`) and variable2 (e.g. `area`), the command needed is:

`CROSSTABS /TABLES sex BY area /STATISTICS 1.`

The output from this command is shown in Figure 14.3 (Chapter 14).

18.3 One-sample chi-square

To find this test in the menu, see Section 18.1 above.

The one-sample chi-square test is used to test a hypothesis such as: *Suicide rate varies significantly from month to month.* If the hypothesis is false, the suicide rate will be the same for every one of the 12 months. The one-sample chi-square is used to compare observed suicide rates per month with what would be expected if the rate were equal for all months. To take an example from exdat, you could test the hypothesis that the number of respondents from the three employers is significantly different from what would be expected if each had contributed an equal number of respondents to the pool. The result is shown in Figure 18.1, which was produced with this command file:

```
GET /FILE 'a:exl.sys'.
SET /LISTING 'a:ex.lis'.
NPAR TESTS /CHISQUARE employer.
```

```
 - - - - - Chi-square Test

     EMPLOYER
                    Cases
     Category  Observed  Expected  Residual
         1        8       7.33       .67
         2        8       7.33       .67
         3        6       7.33      -1.33
                  --
     Total       22

         Chi-Square          D.F.        Significance
            .364               2             .834
```

Figure 18.1: Output from the command NPAR TESTS /CHISQUARE employer.

The categories of employer are listed, with the number of cases for each *(cases observed)*. The expected frequencies which would occur if all employers had had an equal number of cases is shown in the column headed *Expected*. The *Residual* column shows the difference between the observed and the expected values. The final lines show the value of chi-square, the degrees of freedom *(df)* and the probability level.

In this example, chi-square is not significant, as the probability (0.834) is larger than .05.

18.4 Non-parametric tests for matched groups: The Wilcoxon test

To find this test in the menu, see Section 18.1 above.

This test is used to compare the scores of one group of subjects on two variables (a within-subjects comparison), or to compare the scores of two matched groups of respondents on a variable. For example, we may wish to test whether the scores of our exdat respondents on the att1 variable are different from their scores on att2. To use the Wilcoxon test, the command line needed is:

NPAR TESTS /WILCOXON variable1 variable2.

For our problem, the line is:

NPAR TESTS /WILCOXON att1 att2.

The result of this command is shown in Figure 18.2. The Wilcoxon test yields a z value, and this together with the relevant probability level is provided in the output.

```
- - - - - Wilcoxon Matched-pairs Signed-ranks Test

      ATT1
with ATT2
      Mean Rank    Cases
          8.50        3   - Ranks  (ATT2 Lt ATT1)
          9.11       14   + Ranks  (ATT2 Gt ATT1)
                       5     Ties   (ATT2 Eq ATT1)
                      --
                      22    Total

          Z =   -2.4142          2-tailed P =   .0158
```

Figure 18.2: Output from the command NPAR TESTS /WILCOXON att1 att2.

In this instance, probability is less than .05, so you can conclude there is a significant difference between the scores on att1 and att2.

18.5 Non-parametric tests for matched groups: The Friedman test

To find this test in the menu, see Section 18.1.

The Friedman test is used to compare the scores on a particular variable of three or more matched groups. The relevant command line is:

NPAR TESTS /FRIEDMAN variable1 variable2 variable3.

To compare the scores of the exdat respondents on att1, att2 and att3, the Friedman test is required since there are three conditions, and a within-subjects comparison:

NPAR TESTS /FRIEDMAN att1 att2 att3.

The result of this command is shown in Figure 18.3. It gives the mean rank on each variable and a chi-square statistic, degrees of freedom and significance (probability) level. In Figure 18.3, the significance value is less than .05 and so you would conclude there is a significant difference between the scores on the three variables.

```
- - - - - Friedman Two-way ANOVA

Mean Rank    Variable
     1.55    ATT1
     2.14    ATT2
     2.32    ATT3

     Cases        Chi-Square      D.F.   Significance
        22           7.1818         2          .0276
```

Figure 18.3: Output from the command NPAR TESTS /FRIEDMAN att1 att2 att3.

18.6 Non-parametric tests for independent groups: Mann-Whitney

To find this test in the menu, see Section 18.1 above.

Mann-Whitney is used for comparing two independent groups on a specified variable. The general form of the command is:

`NPAR TESTS /MANN-WHITNEY variable1 BY variable2(x,y).`

In the Mann-Whitney command, you use `BY variable2(x,y)` to form two groups based on their scores (x and y) on the variable named as `variable2`.

For example, to compare the sales of respondents from employer 1 and employer 3 in exdat, the command is:

`NPAR TESTS /MANN-WHITNEY sales BY employer(1,3).`

The result of this command is shown in Figure 18.4. Note that the comparison is between those respondents employed by employer 1 and those employed by employer 3. The table contains the mean rank of the two sets of scores, a value for U and a value for z with the associated two-tailed probability. In this example, the probability is less than .05, and you conclude that there is a significant difference between `sales` for employers 1 and 3.

The Mann-Whitney procedure also carries out the Wilcoxon Rank Sum test, and the output shows the value of W and its associated probability.

```
- - - - - Mann-Whitney U - Wilcoxon Rank Sum W Test

      SALES
   by EMPLOYER
      Mean Rank    Cases
         5.38        8    EMPLOYER = 1
        10.33        6    EMPLOYER = 3
                    ——
                    14    Total

                           EXACT              Corrected for Ties
        U            W    2-tailed P         Z        2-tailed P
       7.0         62.0     .0293         -2.1947        .0282
```

Figure 18.4: Output of the command NPAR TESTS /MANN-WHITNEY sales BY employer(1,3).

18.7 Non-parametric tests for independent groups: Kruskal-Wallis

To find this test in the menu, see Section 18.1.

This test is used when three or more independent groups are to be compared. The relevant command is:

NPAR TESTS /KRUSKAL-WALLIS variable1 BY variable2 (x, z) .

In the Kruskal-Wallis test, you use BY variable2 (x, z) to form three or more groups based on their scores on the variable named as variable2. For example, BY employer(1,3) tells SPSS/PC+ to compare the scores on variable1 of the three employer groups whose minimum code number is 1 and maximum code number is 3.

In exdat, for example, to compare the groups from the three different employers in terms of customer visits (cust), the command is:

NPAR TESTS /KRUSKAL-WALLIS cust BY employer(1,3) .

The result of this command is shown in Figure 18.5. The data on customer visits has been ranked, and the mean rank for each employer is given in the table. Two chi-square values are shown below the table, the second having been corrected for tied ranks. Probability values are provided, so in Figure 18.5 you can see that there is a significant difference between the customer visits of the three employers, as the probability value (.0040) is less than .05.

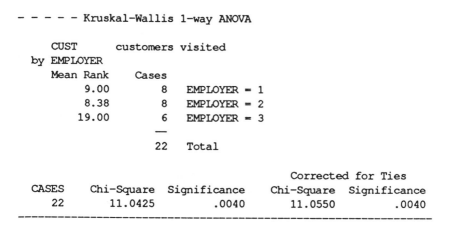

```
- - - - - Kruskal-Wallis 1-way ANOVA

     CUST        customers visited
  by EMPLOYER
     Mean Rank     Cases
         9.00          8    EMPLOYER = 1
         8.38          8    EMPLOYER = 2
        19.00          6    EMPLOYER = 3
                      --
                      22    Total

                                      Corrected for Ties
  CASES    Chi-Square  Significance   Chi-Square  Significance
   22        11.0425         .0040      11.0550         .0040
```

Figure 18.5: Output from the command NPAR TESTS /KRUSKAL-WALLIS cust BY employer(1,3).

18.8 Ranking

To find RANK in the menu, select modify data or files, *go right, from the submenu select* modify data values *and go right again.*

To have the scores on a variable ranked, with the lowest score having a rank of 1, the appropriate command is:

`RANK variable-name.`

To have the scores ranked in descending order, so that the highest score has the rank of 1, select *order* from the RANK submenu, and select *(D)* so the line is:

`RANK variable-name (D).`

If the (D) subcommand is included, all the variables named before that subcommand will be ranked in descending order. To have one variable ranked in ascending order and another in descending order, make this clear by using:

`RANK variable1 (A) variable2 (D).`

Here `variable1` will be in ascending order, because it is followed by (A), and `variable2` will be in descending order.

To rank the data on `sales` in exdat, you would use:

`RANK sales.`

RANK creates a new variable, which by default has the name of the variable being ranked preceded by R. So when `sales` are ranked, you obtain a new variable called `rsales`. This variable name must be used if you wish to list or analyse the ranked values, so to LIST the results of the RANK `sales` command, the command is:

`LIST id rsales.`

The result is shown in Figure 18.6.

The first section shows that the variable sales has been ranked, and the new variable created by the ranking is `rsales`. Its label is *rank of sales*. The output then shows the `rsales` scores for each respondent.

You can specify a new variable name for the ranked data, so that it has a name other than (in this example) `rsales`. This is achieved with:

`RANK variable /RANK INTO newname.`

An example of how this operates is included in Exercise 18.1.

There are a number of options on how to assign ranks to tied values. Unless you specify otherwise, using the /TIES subcommand, tied values will be given the mean rank value of the scores.

The basic RANK command ranks the whole set of scores on the variables named. You frequently need the ranking of scores within subgroups; for example, you may

```
From        New
variable    variable    Label
--------    --------    -----
 SALES       RSALES     RANK of SALES

ID      RSALES
 1        4.000
 2       10.000
 3       22.000
 4       18.000
 5       14.000
 6       15.000
 7        6.000
 8        5.000
 9       11.000
10       17.000
11        9.000
12        1.000
13       21.000
14        2.000
15        8.000
16       20.000
17        3.000
18       16.000
19       19.000
20       12.000
21        7.000
22       13.000

Number of cases read =   22    Number of cases listed =   22
-----------------------------------------------------------------
```

Figure 18.6: Output from the commands RANK sales. and LIST id rsales.

require the data for males and females to be ranked separately. This is achieved using the command:

`RANK variable1 BY variable2.`

To rank the sales figures of the males separately from the ranking of the females' sales figures in exdat, you need this command:

`RANK sales BY sex.`

The output in Figure 18.7 shows the ranking of sales for men and women separately. To have all the males' data appear before the females', the SORT command (described in detail in Section 20.5) was used. The table was produced with the LIST

```
ID SEX    RSALES
 2   1     5.000
 3   1    10.000
 4   1     8.000
 8   1     3.000
 9   1     6.000
10   1     7.000
12   1     1.000
13   1     9.000
17   1     2.000
21   1     4.000
 1   2     2.000
 6   2     8.000
 7   2     3.000
11   2     5.000
14   2     1.000
15   2     4.000
16   2    11.000
18   2     9.000
19   2    10.000
20   2     6.000
22   2     7.000
 5   3     1.000
```

Number of cases read = 22   Number of cases listed = 22

Figure 18.7: Extract of output from the commands RANK sales BY sex. SORT sex. LIST id sex rsales.

command; note that the variable listed was rsales, the new variable created when sales was ranked. The complete set of procedure commands was:

```
RANK sales BY sex.
SORT sex.
LIST id sex rsales.
```

You may wish to rank a variable twice in one program run. For example, in Exercise 18.1, cust is ranked overall and then ranked again by employer. The first ranking will create the variable named rcust; the second time cust is ranked, another default name will be created (ran001), but it is more informative to specify the name for the ranked cust scores on the second rank command using the RANK.../RANK INTO subcommand. Exercise 18.1 includes this naming procedure to illustrate how the process operates.

18.9 Rank Correlation

To obtain a rank correlation between two variables, it is necessary to rank the variables and then use the CORRELATIONS command (Section 17.1) as in this example, which calculates the rank correlation between cust (number of customers visited) and sales:

```
RANK cust sales.
CORRELATIONS /VARIABLES rcust rsales.
```

Note that the correlation command uses the names of the ranked variables, rcust and rsales.

Exercise 18.1

Create the following command file, and save it as excom9:

```
GET /FILE 'a:ex1.sys'.
SET /LISTING 'a:ex9.lis'.
NPAR TESTS /MANN-WHITNEY sales BY sex(1,2).
RANK cust sales.
CORRELATIONS /VARIABLES rcust rsales.
RANK cust BY employer /RANK INTO rnkbyem.
SORT employer.
LIST id employer rnkbyem.
```

Run this file to check whether there is a significant difference between the sales of men and women, to find the rank correlation between customer visits and sales and to obtain a list of ranked customer visits for each employer. The output is shown in Appendix A.

19

Modifying the Data

19.1 Introduction

This chapter explains how to change the way data is coded, so for example all those respondents from exdat who scored over 40 on customer visits can be merged to form one group. It also deals with calculating a new variable from the data; for example, from respondents' sales and the number of customers visited, you can create a new variable which is the average sales per customer visit. It also explains how to select subgroups from the total set of respondents and how to sort cases into a different order.

19.2 Changing the way data is coded and grouping data

Sometimes you may want to code the data in a different way from that used when the data file was initially created. For example, the exdat file includes data on the number of customers visited. You may want to divide the respondents into just two groups: those who visited more than 40 customers, and those who visited less than 40.

Another common situation is when you want to reverse the scoring of one of the variables. For example, in the Sales Personnel Questionnaire described in Chapter 6, there were three questions asking respondents about their attitude to their job. Questions 5 and 6 (named as att1 and att2 in the SPSS/PC+ file) have the responses coded so that 1 indicates the respondent is very satisfied and 5 indicates dissatisfaction. But for question 7 (att3 in the SPSS file), 1 indicates dissatisfaction and 5 indicates satisfaction. Suppose you wanted the scores on att3 to be scored in the opposite direction, so they are consistent with att1 and att2, with a low score meaning very satisfied and a high score (5) meaning very dissatisfied. This kind of alteration is easily made using the RECODE command.

19.3 RECODE

Find RECODE *in the menu by selecting* modify data or files *from the main menu, going right, selecting the* modify data values *option and going right again.*

The general form of the RECODE command involves specifying the variable to be recoded, and then giving formulae to indicate which 'old' scores should be recoded as which 'new' scores. An example is probably the easiest way of explaining how RECODE operates. To modify the exdat data so that two groups are formed according to their standing on the cust scores, insert into the command file the following line:

```
RECODE cust (0 THRU 40 = 1 ) (41 THRU HI = 2) .
```

This puts everyone with a customers visited score of 0 to 40 inclusive into group 1, and everyone with a score of 41 or more into group 2. The expression HI means the highest score on the variable. The equivalent term for the lowest score is LO, so (0 THRU 40 = 1) could have been (LO THRU 40 = 1) .

The second example involves modifying the scores on the att3 variable, the responses to question 7 in the Sales Personnel Questionnaire. We want a score of 5 to be changed to 1, a score of 4 to be changed to 2 and so on, so that the scores are the reverse of the way they were originally encoded. This can be achieved with this command:

```
RECODE att3 (5=1) (4=2) (2=4) (1=5) .
```

After stating the variable to be recoded, simple formulae indicate the existing value and the new value. In this example the previous value of 5 is transformed to 1, 4 becomes 2, 2 becomes 4 and 1 becomes 5. (It is not necessary to recode 3, since it stays as 3.)

If a number of variables are to be recoded, they can be put on a single line, separated by / as in this example:

```
RECODE cust (LO THRU 40 = 1) (41 THRU HI = 2) /att3 (5=1) (4=2) (2=4) (1=5) .
```

So far we have just used RECODE for integers. With non-integers, (which have figures after the decimal point) the task is only slightly more difficult. Imagine you want to recode respondents' sales so that 0 to 3999.99 is a 3, 4000 to 7999.99 is a 2, and anything over 8000 is a 1. If you use RECODE sales (0 THRU 3999 =3) (4000 THRU 7999 =2) (8000 THRU HI = 1), a figure of 7999.50 would not be recoded because it falls between the limits specified; it is more than 7999 but less than 8000. The answer is to reverse the order in which the recoding is specified so the command is:

```
RECODE sales (8000 THRU HI = 1) (4000 THRU 8000 = 2) (LO THRU 4000 =3) .
```

You might imagine that this would cause problems, because the first instruction tells the program to recode 8000 as a 1 and the second tells it to recode 8000 as 2. But any value given in a RECODE line is only operated upon once; so any values of 8000 will be recoded as 1 by the first instruction. When the program comes to the second instruction there will be no values of 8000 for it to find, but all values up to 8000 (including 7999.50) will be available to be recoded as 2.

RECODE only applies to the data when it has been brought into the active file. The original data file is not affected by running the RECODE command, so there is no risk of making permanent (and non-reversible) changes to the entries in the data file. To store a copy of the data to which the RECODE has been applied, carry out the recode, and then save a .SYS file, as explained in Chapter 12.

Exercise 19.1

Create a command file, excom10, that will recode the scores on the `sales` variable in exdat to form two groups. Group 1 has `sales` of less than 7000, and group 2 has `sales` of 7000 or more.

An example that will do this and list the results is given in Appendix A.

19.4 AUTORECODE

Find AUTORECODE *in the menu by selecting* modify data or files *from the main menu, going right, select* modify data values *and go right again.*

This command is similar to RECODE, but it automatically recodes all the scores on a variable into consecutive integers. For example, the customers visited scores in exdat include a 28, a 29, a 30, a 33 and the largest figure is 83. Using AUTORECODE, the scores will be modified so that the lowest score is changed to 1, the second-lowest to 2, the third-lowest to 3 and so on. The command line for achieving this data modification is:

```
AUTORECODE /VARIABLES variable-name /INTO new-variable-name.
```

When the autorecoding takes place, a new variable is created; it has to be named in the /INTO section of the command. Adding the /PRINT subcommand gives a table showing the original scores and the autorecoded scores.

Fig 19.1 shows the effect of running this command file:

```
GET /FILE 'a:ex1.sys'.
SET /LISTING 'a:ex.lis'.
AUTORECODE /VARIABLES cust /INTO newcust /PRINT.
```

The original scores on cust are shown in the *Old Value* column, the AUTORECODEd scores on newcust are shown in the second column. By default, the value labels on the new variable (newcust) are the original variable's values, as is shown in the third column of Figure 19.1. There are only 20 values of newcust, since the original 22 sets of data (Table 6.1) has only 20 different values of cust.

CUST Old Value	NEWCUST New Value	customers visited Value Label
28	1	28
30	2	30
33	3	33
36	4	36
38	5	38
39	6	39
40	7	40
41	8	41
42	9	42
43	10	43
46	11	46
48	12	48
58	13	58
60	14	60
68	15	68
71	16	71
72	17	72
76	18	76
79	19	79
83	20	83

Figure 19.1: Output from the command AUTORECODE /VARIABLES cust /INTO newcust /PRINT.

19.5 Calculating a new score from the data: COMPUTE

To find COMPUTE *in the menu, select* modify data or files, *go right, select* modify data values *and go right again.*

Often, you will want to calculate a new score from the data. This task is achieved with the COMPUTE command, which has the general form:

```
COMPUTE newvariable = variable1+mathematical operator+variable2.
```

For example, in the exdat file, there are scores on customers visited (cust) and on sales. To calculate the average sales per customer visited for each respondent, use compute as here:

COMPUTE salcus = sales/cust.

This tells SPSS/PC+ to compute a new score for each case, the new score to be known as salcus. In this example, it is calculated by dividing sales by cust. The name for the new variable or score must be a new one, i.e. one not already used in the data file. And of course the equation must indicate how the new variable is calculated from existing variables.

In computing a new variable, you can use the usual arithmetic operators: + - * / and ** for exponentiation. (So cust**2 represents the square of cust.) You can also use the square root, the absolute value of a score, the value rounded to the nearest whole number, or the integer value of a non-integer. These and other transformations are obtained by selecting the *!instructions* submenu from the COMPUTE menu, and then selecting the *functions* submenu.

The order in which the formula to the right of the = sign is evaluated follows the conventional rules. Exponentiation is performed first, then multiplication and division, then addition and subtraction. Use brackets to force calculation in the order required. For example, the average score (avatt) of the responses to questions att1, att2 and att3 is computed by this command:

COMPUTE avatt = (att1 + att2 + att3)/3.

A different (and incorrect!) result would of course be given by:

COMPUTE avatt = att1 + att2 +att3/3.

When the COMPUTE line has been inserted into the command file, the new variable can be used in subsequent analyses. So you could go on with:

FREQUENCIES /VARIABLES avatt.

19.6 Missing values in COMPUTE

To find VALUE ( ) *from the* COMPUTE *submenu, select* !instructions *and go right, select* functions *and go right again.*

You will recall that you can specify that a particular value of a variable in the data file means that data is missing; for example, 1 = male 2 = female and 3 = sex not known. Here 3 is the missing value for the sex variable. If any case has a missing value for the variables mentioned in the COMPUTE instruction, the new variable will not be calculated. So if you asked for:

COMPUTE newval = sex + employer.

this would not be calculated for those cases where sex = 3. It is possible to over-ride this, however, by using:

`COMPUTE newval = VALUE(sex) + VALUE(employer).`

When VALUE is applied, the values given to the variables named (sex, employer) are used to compute newval even if they are missing values (such as the score of 3 on sex).

19.7 Computing a new variable with IF

To find IF in the menu, select modify data or files, *go right, select* modify data values *and go right again.* IF *is in the submenu then revealed.*

There are occasions when you may want to compute a variable only if some other condition is fulfilled. Again, this is readily accomplished:

`IF (sales GT 7000) ok=1.`

takes each case and checks to see whether sales is greater than (GT) 7000. If it is, a new variable (ok) is assigned the value of 1. Note that the expression before = must be in brackets.

Use AND, OR, NOT to make the conditional more precise:

`IF (sales GT 7000 AND sex EQ 1) manok=1.`

gives the variable manok the value of 1 if sales is greater than 7000 and the respondent has a sex value of 1.

When evaluating the IF expression, NOT is evaluated first, AND is evaluated before OR.

After creating a new variable using COMPUTE or the conditional transformation IF, it can be given a variable label and value labels as with any other variable. But these commands must occur after the variables have been defined. For example:

`COMPUTE salcus = (sales)/(cust).`
`VARIABLE LABELS salcus 'Average sales per customer visit'.`

Note that the transformations carried out by the commands RECODE, COMPUTE, IF only apply to the data when it has been brought into the active file and is being processed. The original data file (stored on the floppy) is not changed. To transform the data in ways described here and keep a file of the transformed data, it is necessary to save a system file (Chapter 12) as in this example:

```
GET /FILE 'a:ex1.sys'.
COMPUTE avatt = (att1 + att2 +att3)/3.
RECODE cust (LO THRU 40 = 1) (41 THRU HI = 2) /att3 (5=1) (4=2) (2=4)
(1=5).
SAVE /OUTFILE 'a:revex.sys'.
```

If this set of commands is run, the file revex.sys is saved on the floppy disk. Its contents are found using this series of commands:

```
GET /FILE 'a:revex.sys'.
SET /LISTING 'a:ex12.lis'.
LIST.
```

Exercise 19.2

Create a command file, excom11. to compute the new variable newv1, the sum of the scores on att1 and att2, and list the result.

A command file that fulfils these requirements is shown in Appendix A.

19.8 Dealing with dates: YRMODA

YRMODA *is deep in the menu system. To find it, start at the top-level main menu and select and go right at each of these points:* modify data or files, modify data values, COMPUTE, !instructions, *and* functions. *Scroll to the bottom of the submenu to find* YRMODA.

This function converts a date into the number of days since October 15, 1582. While this may appear at first sight somewhat useless, it does in fact allow you to calculate the interval between two dates, such as determining the age of respondents from their date of birth. In exdat, we have the respondents' date of starting their job, recorded as dtsd (which gives the day), dstm (which gives the month) and dsty (which gives the year). Imagine that on June 1st, 1995 we want to calculate tenure, the time for which each respondent has been doing their job. How can we do it?

We need the difference (in years) between the date the respondent started the job and June 1st, 1995. Using the YRMODA function, the number representing June 1st, 1995 is YRMODA(1995,6,1), and that for the respondent's job-start date is given by YRMODA(dsty,dstm,dtsd). (Note that as the name suggests, YRMODA needs dates in the order year-month-day.) So we can find the difference in years with this command:

```
COMPUTE TENURE = (YRMODA(1995,6,1) - YRMODA(dsty,dstm,dtsd)) / 365.35.
```

The result of using this command is shown in Figure 19.2.

```
ID    TENURE
 1     7.00
 2     4.98
 3     4.98
 4     5.00
 5     4.98
 6     4.98
 7     5.00
 8     4.98
 9     4.98
10     4.98
11     4.98
12     5.00
13     3.99
14     3.99
15     3.99
16     4.00
17     3.99
18     4.00
19     3.99
20     4.00
22     4.99

Number of cases read =  22    Number of cases listed =  22
----------------------------------------------------------------
```

Fig 19.2 Output from the commands COMPUTE TENURE = (YRMODA(1995,6,1) - YRMODA(dsty,dstm,dtsd)) / 365.35. and LIST id tenure.

The data on tenure obtained with this command is only present in the active file, and is not stored on the floppy. To have a permanent copy of this data, save a .SYS file, as described in Chapter 12.

19.9 Changing names of variables: MODIFY VARS

To find MODIFY VARS in the menu, select read or write data and go right.

There may be occasions when you want to alter the names of the variables in the file. There are two ways of doing this. One is to edit the DATA LIST FILE line of the original command file and replace the unwanted variable name with another. (If you are using a .SYS file, you will have to create a new one that includes the name change.) Alternatively, use MODIFY VARS like this:

```
MODIFY VARS /RENAME (variable1 = newname).
```

This will rename `variable1` as `newname`. The effect of MODIFY VARS is on the active file, not on the files saved on your disk, so is lost when you leave SPSS/PC+, unless you save a .SYS file.

19.10 Rounding numbers

The data file contains columns of figures, some of which may be decimals. You can round the numbers to any required number of decimal places by marking the rectangle (see Section 8.9), and then pressing F8 and selecting the *Round* entry from the minimenu. Type in the number of decimal places required and press (R) .

20

Selecting Subgroups for Analysis

20.1 Selecting subgroups: SELECT IF

To find SELECT IF *in the menu, select* modify data or files, *go right, select* select or weight data *and go right again.*

You may frequently wish to perform an analysis on a subset of the cases. You tell SPSS/PC+ to select only certain types of case by using:

```
SELECT IF (variable-name+condition+score).
```

Using the data in exdat as an example, suppose you want to compare (using a t-test) the sales scores of men and women but only for those respondents who worked in the North of the country (area = 1). To select respondents from the North, i.e who have an area score of 1, use:

```
SELECT IF (area EQ 1).
```

This command tells the program to select just those cases where the respondent reported working in area 1, and would have to be put before the line asking for the t-test. So the complete set of commands would be:

```
GET /FILE 'a:ex1.sys'.
SET /LISTING 'a:ex.lis'.
SELECT IF (area EQ 1).
T-TEST /GROUPS sex(1,2) /VARIABLES sales.
```

These condition operators can be used to select certain subgroups:

EQ or = mean 'equal to'
GT or > mean 'greater than'
LT or < mean 'less than'

NE or <> mean 'not equal to'
LE or <= mean 'less than or equal to'
GE or >= mean 'more than or equal to'

To get a subset of respondents who had any employer other than 1, use:

`SELECT IF (employer NE 1).`

Note that SELECT IF continues to operate for the rest of the run. For example, if we select just the females from the data file using `SELECT IF (sex = 2)`, and do some analysis on the female's scores, we cannot then use `SELECT IF (area = 2)` to pick out everyone, male or female, from area 2. If we have `SELECT IF (sex = 2)` and then `SELECT IF (area = 2)`, our selected group is now females of area 2. This might not be what is wanted. We may want to select just the females to do one analysis, and then select Southern area subjects of either sex for a second analysis. This can be done, but requires the use of PROCESS IF rather than SELECT IF.

20.2 Selecting subgroups: PROCESS IF

To find PROCESS IF *in the menu, select* modify data or files, *go right, select* select or weight data *and go right again.*

This command works just like SELECT IF *except* that it is only in effect for one following procedure. So you could analyse just the males and then just the females like this:

```
PROCESS IF (sex = 1).
CROSSTABS /TABLES employer BY area.
PROCESS IF (sex=2).
CROSSTABS /TABLES employer BY area.
```

If SELECT IF had been used in this example, it would not work. As you would have selected only the cases where sex = 1 in the first line, the third line would not be able to find any cases which matched the criterion of having sex = 2.

The example just given is not in practice the way you would normally obtain a CROSSTABS of employer by area for each sex separately; the simpler way of achieving that is to use:

`CROSSTABS /TABLES employer BY area BY sex.`

Exercise 20.1

Create a command file, excom12, which will show the mean score on att3 only for those respondents who scored 1 on att1, and then gives a frequency table of the responses on att2 only for respondents working in the South (area 2).

A command file that does this is given in Appendix A.

20.3 Selecting a random sample of cases: SAMPLE

To find SAMPLE *in the menu, select* modify data or files, *go right, select* select or weight data *and go right again.*

With very large data file, you may wish to select a sample of cases for analysis. To select a 10% random sample, use:

SAMPLE 0.10.

A 20% random sample is obtained by:

SAMPLE 0.20.

To obtain a specific number of cases (say 50) selected at random from a data file containing 500 cases, use:

SAMPLE 50 FROM 500.

To obtain a precise number of cases in the sample, you must give the total number of cases in the file after FROM. If you give a number larger than the actual number of cases in the data file, the number requested will be scaled proportionally. For example, the line above asked for 50 cases from 500, a 10% sample. If the file actually had only 400 cases, the SAMPLE command would yield 40 cases, still a 10% sample.

The SAMPLE command is like PROCESS IF in that it is only operative for one following procedure.

20.4 Selecting the first n cases: N

To find N *in the menu, select* modify data or files, *go right, select* select or weight data *and go right again.*

To analyse just the first *n* cases in the data file use:

N 100.

which selects the first 100 cases. N 20 selects the first 20 cases, of course.

20.5 Putting the cases in a different order: SORT

To find SORT *in the menu select* modify data or files, *go right, select* manipulate files *and go right again.*

There are occasions when you may wish to sort the cases into a new order. For example, if you were analysing just the first 50 cases in a large data file, you might want those first 50 cases to be all males, or all of a given level of income or having some other feature. You can have the cases sorted into a specified order using the SORT command, which has the general form:

```
SORT variable-name.
```

In our data file, exdat, males (sex = 1) and females (sex = 2) are distributed throughout the data file. If we want all the males to be listed together, we can use:

```
SORT sex.
```

This sorts the cases according to their value on the sex variable, putting all the cases where sex = 1 (i.e males) before the cases where sex = 2 (the females). If you wished all the females to come first, you would use:

```
SORT sex (D).
```

The (D) tells the program to sort in descending order (so 2 comes before 1).

You may want the cases sorted by two variables, for example by area and by sex. This is achieved by:

```
SORT variable1 variable2.
```

If the (D) order command is included in the line, all the variables named in the line before (D) are sorted in descending order, unless one specifies the use of ascending order with (A).

```
SORT area (A) sex (D).
```

tells the program to sort the variable area in ascending order, the variable sex in descending order.

Figure 20.1 shows the effects of running this command file:

```
GET /FILE 'a:ex1.sys'.
SORT employer (A) sex (D).
LIST employer sex id.
```

```
EMPLOYER SEX ID
       1   2  1
       1   2  7
       1   2 18
       1   2 22
       1   1  3
       1   1  9
       1   1 12
       1   1 17
       2   3  5
       2   2 11
       2   2 14
       2   2 15
       2   2 20
       2   1  2
       2   1  8
       2   1 21
       3   2  6
       3   2 16
       3   2 19
       3   1  4
       3   1 10
       3   1 13
```

Number of cases read =   22   Number of cases listed =   22

Figure 20.1: Output from the commands SORT employer (A) sex (D). LIST employer sex id.

As can be seen, it has re-ordered the cases in the file, sorting by ascending employer number and then putting all the females before the males.

Sorting cases in this way is useful when preparing the data for printing out, as it groups together similar cases (such as all respondents of a given sex or age). It is often needed when using the REPORT command (Section 22.2), and when adding data files together (Chapter 23).

21

Graphs

21.1 Histograms and barcharts

To find FREQUENCIES *and* EXAMINE *in the menu, select* analyze data, *go right, select* descriptive statistics *and go right again.*

Histograms differ from a barcharts in that they will show an empty row where there is no data whereas a barcharts leaves out any empty rows. Both histograms and barcharts are subcommands of the FREQUENCIES procedure:

```
FREQUENCIES /VARIABLES variable-name /HISTOGRAM.
FREQUENCIES /VARIABLES variable-name /BARCHART.
```

In exdat, dsty gives the year in which the respondents started their job. There is no case of anyone starting in 1989, but one person started in 1988, and the rest in 1990

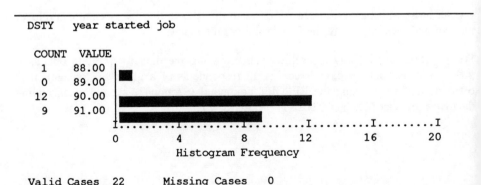

Figure 21.1: Extract of output from the command FREQUENCIES/VARIABLES dsty /HISTOGRAM.

or 1991. The histogram of this data is shown in Figure 21.1 and the barchart in Figure 21.2. As can be seen, the histogram has an empty row corresponding to year 89, while the barchart does not.

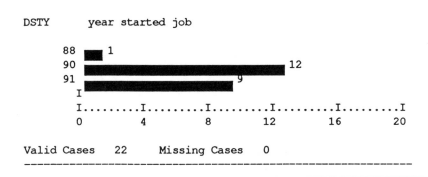

Figure 21.2: Extract of output from the command FREQUENCIES/VARIABLES dsty /BARCHART.

The horizontal scale of histogram or barchart can be percentages rather than frequencies by using:

```
FREQUENCIES /VARIABLES variable-name/HISTOGRAM PERCENT (100).
```

It is also possible to obtain crude histograms from the EXAMINE command, covered in Section 13.4, using:

```
EXAMINE /VARIABLES variable-name /PLOT HISTOGRAM.
```

The output from Exercie 13.1, shown in Appendix A, illustrates the EXAMINE. . . /PLOT output.

21.2 Scattergrams

To find PLOT, select graph data from the main menu and go right; PLOT is in the submenu.

To obtain a simple bivariate scattergram, use PLOT/PLOT and indicate the two variables to be plotted:

```
PLOT /PLOT variable1 WITH variable2.
```

The first variable named is plotted on the vertical axis.

Specify labels for the two axes with:

```
PLOT /VERTICAL 'vertical label' /HORIZONTAL 'horizontal label'
/PLOT variable1 WITH variable2.
```

Replace the phrases within inverted commas with whatever labels are required.

To specify a title for the graph, include /TITLE 'Put the title here', so the complete line is:

```
PLOT /TITLE 'Fig 1' /VERTICAL 'vertical label' /HORIZONTAL 'horizontal label'
/PLOT variable1 WITH variable2.
```

The size of the graph can be altered by specifying the lines down it will occupy (VSIZE) and its width in character spaces (HSIZE) as here:

```
PLOT /VSIZE 30 /HSIZE 40 /PLOT variable1 WITH variable2.
```

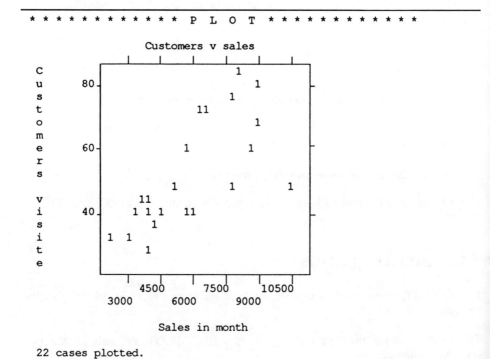

Figure 21.3: Output from the command PLOT /TITLE 'Customers v Sales'
/VERTICAL 'Customers visited' /HORIZONTAL 'Sales in month' /VSIZE 15 /HSIZE
30 /PLOT cust WITH sales.

The graph shown in Figure 21.3 was obtained by combining these subcommands to form this line:

```
PLOT /TITLE 'Customers v Sales' /VERTICAL 'Customers visited' /HORIZONTAL
     'Sales in month' /VSIZE 15 /HSIZE 30 /PLOT cust WITH sales.
```

21.3 Scatterplot with correlation coefficient

To find PLOT, *select* graph data *from the main menu and go right;* PLOT *is in the submenu.*

To find REGRESSION *in the menu, select* analyze data, *go right, select* correlation and regression *and go right again. The* SCATTERPLOT *subcommand is found by selecting* residual analysis *from the* REGRESSION *submenu and going right. Note that the main procedure* REGRESSION *is not to be confused with the* FORMAT REGRESSION *subcommand of the* PLOT *procedure.*

To obtain a scatterplot and measure of correlation, use either PLOT or REGRESSION. The command using the PLOT procedure is:

```
PLOT /FORMAT REGRESSION /PLOT variable1 WITH variable2.
```

(It is not possible to obtain a scattergram from within a CORRELATIONS command line.)

Note that the final /PLOT subcommand must be the last entry in the PLOT line.

An example of this command is given in section 17.2 and the output shown in Figure 17.2.

If you are using the REGRESSION procedure, a number of plotting alternatives are available. A simple scatterplot of the standard scores on variable1 and variable2. is obtained from:

```
REGRESSION /VARIABLES variable1 variable2 /DEPENDENT variable1 /METHOD ENTER
/SCATTERPLOT (variable1 variable2).
```

REGRESSION requires that the variables be stated, the dependent variable be specified and the regression method be given, as in the line shown. (More explanation of REGRESSION is provided in Section 17.3.) Figure 21.4 shows the scatterplot result of using this series of commands:

```
GET /FILE 'a:exl.sys'.
REGRESSION /VARIABLES cust sales /DEPENDENT cust /METHOD ENTER
/SCATTERPLOT (cust sales).
```

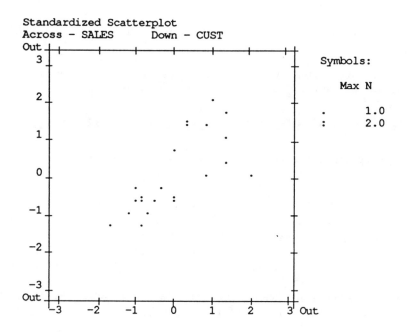

Figure 21.4 Extract of output from the command REGRESSION /VARIABLES cust sales /DEPENDENT cust /METHOD ENTER /SCATTERPLOT (cust sales).

21.4 Stem-leaf plots and boxplots

These are obtained with the EXAMINE procedure, described in Section 13.4.

EXAMINE /VARIABLES variable1.

provides both types of diagram. A stem and leaf plot is similar to a histogram, but numbers indicate the actual values plotted.

Figure 21.5 shows a stem-leaf plot obtained with the commands:

GET /FILE 'a:ex1.sys'.
EXAMINE /VARIABLES cust.

The first column shows the number of scores in the band indicated by the stem. For example, the first line of Figure 21.5 shows there was one respondent who scored in the twenties on customers visited (the stem is 2). The actual score of this respondent was 28 (the leaf is 8, so the actual score is 2, the stem, and 8 the leaf).

A boxplot summarises the scores on a variable by displaying the median (as an asterisk), the 25th and 75th percentiles as the lower and upper edges of a box surrounding the median. The box length represents the interquartile range of the

```
    Frequency      Stem &  Leaf

        1.00       2  .  8
        6.00       3  .  036899
        7.00       4  .  0123688
        1.00       5  .  8
        2.00       6  .  08
        4.00       7  .  1269
        1.00       8  .  3

    Stem width:    10
    Each leaf:       1 case(s)
```

Figure 21.5: Stem-leaf plot from the command EXAMINE /VARIABLES cust.

scores. Outliers are cases which are between 1.5 and 3 boxlengths from the edge of the box, and Extremes are more than 3 boxlengths away. Lines are drawn from the edge of the box to the largest and smallest values which are not outliers. An example is given in Figure 21.6, but for these scores there are no Outliers nor Extremes.

The boxplot allows you to make a number of 'eye-ball' judgements about the distribution of the scores. The median is the indicator of the central value, and the length of the box indicates the variability of the scores. If the median is not in the middle of the box, the distribution of scores is skewed.

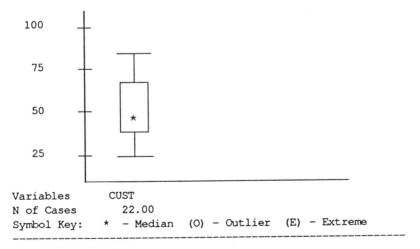

Figure 21.6: Boxplot of cust from the command EXAMINE /VARIABLES cust.

22

Presenting the Printout in the way you want

22.1 Obtaining a clean .LIS file

The results from an SPSS/PC+ analysis are put into the .LIS file, and during a single SPSS/PC+ session, the .LIS file is built up with the results of later runs being added to it. If you wish to use the .LIS file for presenting the results of your analysis, you will need a clean version of the file, containing just the results you want. There are various ways of obtaining a clean .LIS file.

One way is to get the command file perfect, so that it runs without error, and then leave SPSS/PC+, re-enter it from DOS and run the command file. The .LIS file will be started afresh, and only the clean output will then feature in it.

A further method of obtaining a clean .LIS file is to edit it, as described in Section 11.5.

Yet another way of obtaining a clean and tidy printout of the results of your analysis is to use the REPORT procedure.

22.2 Using REPORT

To find REPORT *in the menu system, select* analyze data, *go right, select* reports and tables, *and go right again.*

Figure 22.1 shows the result of a REPORT command and the command lines that were used. REPORT creates tables from the data, and there is a wide variety of formatting commands. It is worth noting that REPORT can be criticised for being too

Customers and sales per salesperson

SEX	ID	customers visited	SALES
male	2	46	4984.42
	3	48	10432.82
	4	83	8235.21
	8	28	3819.00
	9	41	5723.52
	10	76	7937.45
	12	30	2005.30
	13	68	8914.50
	17	38	3449.35
	21	39	4004.80
Sum			59506.37
Mean	10	50	5950.64
female	1	43	3450.60
	6	72	6497.05
	7	42	3835.26
	11	39	4582.44
	14	33	3124.20
	15	36	4222.45
	16	79	8881.28
	18	48	7882.60
	19	58	8779.00
	20	60	5822.68
	22	40	5886.40
Sum			62963.96
Mean	14	50	5724.00
.	5	71	6441.38
Sum			6441.38
Mean	5	71	6441.38

```
GET /FILE 'a:ex1.sys'.
SET /LISTING 'a:ex17.lis'.
SET /LENGTH 70.
SORT sex.
REPORT /FORMAT AUTOMATIC LIST LENGTH (5,65) /VARIABLES id cust
sales /TITLE LEFT 'Customers and sales per salesperson' /BREAK
sex /SUMMARY SUM (sales) /SUMMARY MEAN.
```

Figure 22.1: An example of output from REPORT and the commands used to create it.

flexible: there are so many variations you can use in laying out the table that even the menu help window suggests you may find it easier to type in the commands rather than using the menu! Also, tables can be obtained from other procedures such as CROSSTABS, and the resulting .LIS file edited to achieve a tidy tabular presentation without using REPORT at all.

Since REPORT has such a range of options, only the basic aspects of the command will be described. Once you have tried it out, you can explore further possibilities using the menus and/or the SPSS/PC+ manual.

The REPORT command reads the cases from the data file in sequential order. So it is usually necessary to re-order the data in the active file to put it in the order required to create the table. For example, to have a table showing all the males and then all the females, it is necessary to sort the file so that all the same-sex cases are together. This is done by:

`SORT sex.`

Further details on the SORT procedure are given in Section 20.5.

Once the data has been sorted, the REPORT command can be invoked. It produces tables in which the variables are set in columns, as shown in Figure 22.1. The table can list the variable values for individual cases from the data file, or it can list particular subgroupings of cases. The table can contain summary statistics such as the mean or sum for subgroups of cases. An example should help to make this clear.

In exdat there is data on males and females, and we want to obtain a table listing the sales data for each sex separately, with the means for the two sexes shown.

To obtain a list of the data file's cases, the report line must include a LIST subcommand:

`REPORT /FORMAT AUTOMATIC LIST`

The FORMAT AUTOMATIC entry means that the system uses a set of default formatting instructions. (These can be altered if you use FORMAT MANUAL which invokes a different set of defaults.)

A REPORT command has to indicate which variable or variables are to be shown. To tabulate the id, customers visited and sales for each sex, the line would include:

`REPORT /FORMAT AUTOMATIC LIST /VARIABLES id cust sales`

(The order in which the variables are named determines the sequence of columns in the output table.)

When using REPORT you usually want the table to subdivide the cases into groups (for example into males and females). To specify the variable which is to be used to create the subgroups, use /BREAK followed by the variable name. So to create subgroups based on sex:

`REPORT /FORMAT AUTOMATIC LIST /VARIABLES id cust sales /BREAK sex`

Various summary statistics can be requested including mean, variance, sd, sum, min, max, mode and median, but each must be preceded with the /SUMMARY subcommand. To obtain the totals and means for each of the subgroups, the complete line becomes:

`REPORT /FORMAT AUTOMATIC LIST /VARIABLES id cust sales /BREAK sex /SUMMARY SUM`
`/SUMMARY MEAN .`

To have summary statistics for some of the named variables only, use a line like this:

`REPORT /FORMAT AUTOMATIC LIST /VARIABLES id cust sales /BREAK sex /SUMMARY SUM`
`(sales) /SUMMARY MEAN .`

By default the table will have a title which is the same as the title of the pages in the .LIS file. To give the table its own title use:

`/TITLE 'Title of table'`

The positioning of the title can be centred on the page (the default) or left/right aligned.

`/TITLE LEFT 'Table 1'`

will produce a left-aligned title.

An example that includes all these options is:

`REPORT /FORMAT AUTOMATIC LIST /VARIABLES id cust sales /TITLE LEFT 'Customers`
`and sales per salesperson' /BREAK sex /SUMMARY SUM (sales) /SUMMARY MEAN .`

22.3 Setting REPORT table length for the printer

REPORT will automatically assume that a table can only be as long as the 25 lines used for screen displays. This is inappropriate for printed output, when you want to use the full depth of the paper. You can set the length of the printed table so that it is appropriate for the paper size on your printer, but must first alter the system page length, which is 25 lines unless altered by using a SET command such as:

`SET /LENGTH 70 .`

The number tells the program how many lines there on a page, and 70 is appropriate for A4 paper.

Having set the system page length, you can then incorporate in the REPORT command a subcommand which tells the procedure where to start printing on a page and how long the page is:

```
/FORMAT AUTOMATIC LIST LENGTH (5,65)
```

The 5 tells REPORT to start printing on the fifth line of the page; the 65 tells it to print down to line 65. You should, of course, use the numbers you want in this subcommand. An example of the procedure for obtaining tables from REPORT that fit an A4 sheet is:

```
SET /LENGTH 70.
REPORT /FORMAT AUTOMATIC LIST LENGTH (5,65) /VARIABLES id cust sales
/TITLE LEFT 'Customers and sales per salesperson' /BREAK sex /SUMMARY SUM
(sales) /SUMMARY MEAN.
```

The output is shown in Figure 22.1.

As can be seen, the output does give neat tables. You may have noticed that Figure 22.1 gives the mean of the id values, a nonsensical figure. This could have been avoided by using /SUMMARY MEAN (cust sales) instead of merely /SUMMARY MEAN. You will also see that Figure 22.1 has one case shown by a full-stop in the left-hand column. This is the respondent whose sex is unknown and who therefore cannot be categorized as male or female.

22.4 Sending the output of REPORT to a separate file

When using REPORT, the tables can be sent to a separate file so that they can be printed later by the OUTFILE subcommand. For example, the following sends the results of the REPORT command to a file called rep.lis on the floppy disk (drive a):

```
REPORT /FORMAT AUTOMATIC LIST /VARIABLES sales /OUTFILE 'a:rep.lis' /TITLE
'Table 1' /BREAK sex /SUMMARY SUM .
```

From DOS, the tables can be printed using the usual:

```
type a:rep.lis >prn (R)
```

23

Merging Data Files

23.1 Introduction

You may find that you have two sets of data, in separate files, that you want to merge to form one file. There are two situations where this is likely to happen. First, you have collected data from a sample of respondents, and later obtain data from some more respondents which you want to add to your first set. The obvious way of doing this is to retrieve the original data file and simply add the new cases on the end, but this is not always feasible. (Perhaps you have the data from 1,000 children in Mexico, and a colleague has data from 1,000 children in Poland. Both of you have written a file containing the data you have collected, neither of you wants to type in another 1,000 cases!) You can merge the two data files together using the JOIN ADD command, which is explained below (Section 23.2).

The second situation where you want to merge data is when you have data from a set of respondents, and then obtain another series of responses from the same respondents. For example, imagine we surveyed 500 adults on their alcohol drinking behaviour six months ago and yesterday. We want to add the data we collected yesterday to the file of their responses of six months ago, so we can look at changes in drinking behaviour over the six month period. We are not adding new cases to our data file, only adding new data to existing cases. We could go back and add the new data to our data file, but it may be that we have the two data sets in separate files and want to merge them. For this type of situation, you need the JOIN MATCH procedure (Section 23.4).

23.2 Adding cases: JOIN ADD

To find JOIN ADD *in the menu system, select* modify data or files, *go right, select* manipulate files *and go right again.*

The vital point to note at the outset is that the JOIN procedures can only be used with .SYS files, not ordinary data files. If you have not yet done so, make sure you understand the notion of .SYS files and how to create them (Chapter 12).

The simplest method of explaining how to join data files is to give examples for you to work through. Suppose we have data from three additional respondents to add to our exdat file. This extra data is shown in Figure 23.1. These numbers are rather simple, but this example demonstrates how JOIN ADD works; the techniques apply just as easily to larger data sets.

```
23 1 1 1 3 2 3 055 03800.50 010691
24 2 2 2 4 2 4 060 04780.60 030690
25 2 1 2 3 2 5 078 06782.00 040690
```

Figure 23.1: Additional data from three respondents to be added to exdat

Write a new data file containing the lines shown in Figure 23.1, and save it as dat2 on the floppy disk. To merge this data with the data in exdat, the first task is to create .SYS files of each data set. You have already created a .SYS file (ex1.sys) for exdat (Chapter 12). To create a .SYS file of dat2, use this command file:

```
DATA LIST FILE 'a:dat2' FIXED/id 1-2 sex 4 employer 6 area 8 att1 10 att2
    12 att3 14 cust 16-18 sales 20-27 (2) dstd 29-30 dstm 31-32 dsty 33-34.
SAVE /OUTFILE 'a:dat2.SYS'.
```

Write this command file, save it as dat2com, and run it. It creates a second .SYS file, dat2.sys, which contains the data from the dat2 file.

Now write another command file which merges the two .SYS files together and saves the merged file as ex2.sys. This file can be saved as jacom, and needs to contain these lines:

```
JOIN ADD /FILE 'a:ex1.sys' /FILE 'a:dat2.sys'.
SAVE /OUTFILE 'a:ex2.sys'.
```

This adds the contents of the dat2.sys file to the end of the ex1.sys file so that ex2.sys now contains both sets of data. After running jacom to check that the merge has been successful, write and run another command file, mergcom, which will LIST the cases starting at number 20:

```
GET /FILE 'a:ex2.sys'.
SET /LISTING 'a:merg.lis'.
LIST /CASES FROM 20.
```

If all has gone well, the listing, stored in merg.lis, will be as shown in Figure 23.2.

ID	SEX	EMPLOYER	AREA	ATT1	ATT2	ATT3	CUST	SALES	DSTD	DSTM	DSTY
20	2	2	2	1	3	4	60	5822.68	31	5	91
21	1	2	2	3	4	3	39	4004.80	3	6	91
22	2	1	1	2	3	3	40	5886.40	5	6	90
23	1	1	1	3	2	3	55	3800.50	1	6	91
24	2	2	2	4	2	4	60	4780.60	3	6	90
25	2	1	2	3	2	5	78	6782.00	4	6	90

Number of cases read =   25   Number of cases listed =   6

Figure 23.2: The LIST of cases from 20 onward in ex2.sys, obtained by running mergcom.

As Figure 23.2 shows, the file ex2.sys has the additional three cases from dat2. The data in the joined file is in the order that comes from simply adding one file on to the end of the other. To obtain a different order, perhaps putting all the males (sex=1) together, use the SORT command (Section 20.5). The cases can be stored in their sorted order by saving another .SYS file after the SORT command.

It is possible to join files and drop (delete) some of the variables from one of the files. This is unlikely to be needed by a beginner, and so the procedures will not be described here. They are, of course, described in the SPSS/PC+ Manual.

When joining files, the two data files have to be identical in the way the data is laid out. (The names of the variables id, sex, area and so on need not be the same in the two files being joined, but if they differ the names used in the second file listed in the JOIN command will be the ones used in the joined file.)

23.3 Adding cases using *Insert file*

The SPSS/PC+ manual asserts that you must use .SYS files when joining files. But if you press F3 you will find that the minimenu contains the entry *Insert file*. The section of the manual describing what this does is hard to find, but it does say that this command is for inserting the contents of a DOS file into the current file (i.e. the one in the scratchpad).

It is possible to use this facility for merging data files. If you have two sets of data stored on the floppy disk as normal (i.e. not .SYS) files, and are editing one of these data files, the other can be inserted into it by pressing F3, selecting the *Insert file* option and typing in the name of the file to be inserted. If the combined file is saved, it will be found to have both sets of data. This is somewhat easier than the JOIN ADD procedure described in Section 23.2. The absence of any comment on it in the

ADD procedure described in Section 23.2. The absence of any comment on it in the official manual may imply that there are some limitations to its use, and that it is safer to rely on JOIN ADD.

23.4 Adding scores to existing cases: JOIN MATCH

To find JOIN MATCH *in the menu system, select* modify data or files, *go right, select* manipulate files *and go right again.*

Imagine we have additional data for the respondents recorded in exdat: perhaps we now have their date of birth, as a six-digit number like this: 050870 (5th August, 1970).

This additional data is stored in a data file (addat). An example of the data for the first two respondents is:

```
01 120870
02 221070
```

To add the data to that in the exdat file, you must use the JOIN MATCH command. As with JOIN ADD, you must use .SYS files, so it is necessary to create .SYS files for each of the data sets. The system file for exdat (ex1.sys) already exists on the floppy disk. To obtain a .SYS file for the data file of additional data, you would run a command file like this:

```
DATA LIST FILE 'a:addat' FIXED/ id 1-2 dobd 4-5 dobm 6-7 doby 8-9.
SAVE /OUTFILE 'a:add.SYS'.
```

This creates add.sys, the .SYS file version of the additional file of data. The two sets of data can be merged by writing and running another file containing these commands:

```
JOIN MATCH /FILE 'a:ex1.sys' /FILE 'a:add.sys'.
SAVE /OUTFILE 'a:full.sys'.
```

This creates a merged file formed by adding add.sys to ex1.sys, and saves the merged data as full.sys.

To determine whether the joining of the two files has been successful you would need a command file like this:

```
GET /FILE 'a:full.sys'.
SET /LISTING 'a:full.lis'.
LIST.
```

23.5 JOIN MATCH with incomplete data

The example of JOIN MATCH described in the previous section is simple, because every respondent in exdat and therefore in ex1.sys also appeared in addat and therefore in add.sys. Real data is often not so neat! What happens if you only have the second set of data on some of the respondents?

Suppose we have another set of additional data, which is the marital status of some of our respondents. The variable is named as marst, and 1 means unmarried, 2 is married. The data is shown in Figure 23.3, the first two digits being the respondent's id. Write this data file and save it on your floppy disk as setxdat.

```
06 1
03 2
05 2
18 1
11 2
```

Figure 23.3: Additional data (setxdat) on the respondents in exdat to be added to the exdat file

Setxdat has scores on marst for five respondents. (Note that in setxdat the respondents are not in the same order as in the original data file; this is so you see how to cope with this situation.)

When you merge the data from the two files, it is obviously essential that the data from setxdat is added to the appropriate person in exdat. There must be some way of identifying which lines from exdat match which lines from setxdat, and in this example id lets us do that because it is included in both the data files.

The first step is to create .SYS files for each of the data files. We have ex1.sys, the .SYS file of exdat. To create a .SYS file for the setxdat file, write and run this command file (setcom):

```
DATA LIST FILE 'a:setxdat' FIXED/ id 1-2 marst 4.
SAVE /OUTFILE 'a:setx.sys'.
```

We now have on the floppy ex1.sys, the .SYS file of exdat, and setx.sys which is the .SYS file of setxdat. To merge the data, it is essential to make sure the data for respondent 05 from setx.sys is added to the data for that same subject from ex.sys, and similarly for the other respondents. We need therefore to match the data from the two files by id, and the first thing is to sort the cases into ascending order of id.

For ex1.sys this is already done; the data starts with respondent 01 and goes up to respondent 22 in ascending order. But for setx.sys, it is not in the correct order. So the next task is to put it in ascending order by writing and running this command file (sosetcom):

```
GET /FILE 'a:setx.sys'.
SORT id.
SAVE /OUTFILE 'a:setx.asf'.
```

This creates another .SYS file (setx.asf) of the data in setxdat with the cases in ascending order of id.

The two sets of data can now be joined, and the result listed, by writing and running this command file (jm2com):

```
JOIN MATCH /FILE 'a:ex1.sys' /FILE 'a:setx.asf'/BY id.
SAVE /OUTFILE 'a:mat.sys'.
```

ID	SEX	MARST
1	2	.
2	1	.
3	1	2
4	1	.
5	3	2
6	2	1
7	2	.
8	1	.
9	1	.
10	1	.
11	2	2
12	1	.
13	1	.
14	2	.
15	2	.
16	2	.
17	1	.
18	2	1
19	2	.
20	2	.
21	1	.
22	2	.

Number of cases read = 22   Number of cases listed = 22

Figure 23.4: The output of the command LIST id sex marst. applied to mat.sys.

The first line tells SPSS/PC+ which two files to merge (note that for setx it is setx.asf, the file which has the data sorted into an ascending sequence based on id). It also, using BY id, tells SPSS/PC+ to merge data according to id so that the data for respondent 05 in ex1.sys is matched to that from subject 05 in setx.asf.

The second line saves a new .SYS file (mat.sys) that contains the merged data.

To confirm that the new data has been added to the correct lines of the original data, you can LIST mat.lis. The output from the command LIST id sex marst. is shown in Figure 23.4, and demonstrates that the new data has been paired with the correct respondent.

24

Designing your Research for SPSS/PC+ Analysis

24.1 Designing a response form

SPSS/PC+ makes it possible to analyse large sets of data in very brief time, once the data file has been created. It is especially useful for analysing the results of surveys, where each of a large number of respondents may yield a large amount of data. It is sensible to consider, when designing a survey response form, the person who is going to have to type the responses into a data file. This job of keying the data into a data file can be a large task in its own right, and the researcher can produce some gains by designing the response forms from the outset so that keying the data is made as easy as possible. This involves two aspects of form design: first, asking questions in such a way that the respondent gives clear and unambiguous responses; second, laying the form out so that the keyboard operator has as straightforward a task as possible.

Designing questionnaires that are effective is not a simple job, and the first attempt is almost never the optimal solution. Questionnaires should always be piloted, given to a small sample of people of the same type that are to be given the final version, so that any ambiguities or mistakes can be identified and corrected before the form is given to the final users. There are a number of simple rules that the questionnaire designer should follow, although experience suggests that even those who know what the rules are find it very difficult to implement them (which is why a pilot study is always necessary!).

Questions should be unambiguous, and ambiguity is not always apparent to the person who devises the questions. For example, *"Are you aged over 65?"* may seem clear, but many ordinary people who are 65 may be unsure how to respond. Does the question mean *"Have you had your 65th birthday?"* or does it mean *"Are you aged 66 or more?"*

Ambiguity is more likely if the question setter makes the mistake of combining clauses. For example, you should not use questions like this: *"Are you a fluent speaker of English and Spanish?"* It is better to use separate questions, each with a yes/no possibility.

People find it more difficult to interpret negatives and passive sentences than positives and active sentences. It is wise to avoid such questions as: *"Do not fill in this form if you are aged under 16"*; it is preferable to use the positive equivalent: *"Fill in this form if you are aged 16 or over"*.

Imprecise terms such as *often* and *frequently* are inherently ambiguous. A question such as: *"Do you often have sleepless nights?"* is unlikely to produce clear answers, since the respondents concept of *often* may not correspond with the questioner's - does it mean once a week, once a month, once a year? The term *sleepless night* is also unclear - does it mean literally having no sleep at all, or being awake for two or more hours after trying to go to sleep?

The kind of response required also influences the way people answer questions. One should avoid having respondents 'delete whichever does not apply'; instead, have them tick or underline or circle the alternative that does apply. This is another aspect of avoiding negatives, and is particularly important if there is any risk of presenting the respondent with a double negative as here: *"Delete whichever does not apply....I am over 16 / I am not over 16."*

When offering alternative answers, one must be sure that all possible answers are offered, even if this means allowing the respondent to write in a response not catered for. If asking about people's marital status, you must allow for the separated, the divorced, the widowed, and (depending on the purpose of the research) for those living together on a long-term basis who are not legally married, know how to code the response if the respondent ticks two or more of the alternatives.

The completed forms are going to be transformed into a data file, so it is important to arrange the design so that the keyboard operator has a clear task. Most, if not all, responses will be transformed into numbers, so the numbers corresponding to each question and each response must be known in advance, and it can be helpful to have them indicated on the form or to provide a template which can be used when the keying is being done. It is important to ensure that the responses to any question are placed in the appropriate columns of the data file, that a failure to respond is indicated by a number, that allowance has been made for multiple answers and free responses.

Answers should be clearly located next to the questions, and questions clearly differentiated from the adjacent ones. Although having alternative responses arranged in columns does save paper, a set of similar rows is likely to cause keyboard operators to lose their place, with the danger that the responses to one question may be keyed in as the responses to a different question.

24.2 Numeric and string (alphanumeric) variables

SPSS/PC+ does accept alphanumeric (known as string) data, in which the data is coded in the data file not as a number but as a series of letters (or letters and numbers). If the data contains any letters, it is a string variable. SPSS/PC+ divides string variables into two types: short ones, which have eight characters or less, and long ones.

If you are using string variables in your data file, you have to tell SPSS/PC+ that the variable is a string variable in the DATA LIST line by adding (A) after the variable name:

`DATA LIST FILE = 'a:smoke.dat'/id 1-3 brand 5-15(A) age 17-20.`

Here id and age are numeric, but brand is a string variable.

There are some drawbacks to using alphanumeric variables. First, typing in strings takes longer than typing in numbers. Second, there are limitations on what you can do with string variables: you cannot use them in most of the statistical procedures that SPSS/PC+ offers. Consequently, it is more convenient to use numerical coding of all variables. The VALUE LABELS command allows you to obtain in the printout a verbal label corresponding to any numerical score.

It is possible to transform string variables into numeric ones by a slightly indirect method. Suppose, for example, that you have a data file in which sex has been coded as M, F or U (for *unknown*). You can create a new numeric variable, gender, which codes sex as a number by using the IF procedure:

```
IF (sex = 'M') gender = 1.
IF (sex = 'F') gender = 2.
IF (sex = 'U') gender = 3.
```

Gender is a numeric variable and can be used in FREQUENCIES, DESCRIPTIVES and the other procedures which require numeric variables.

As was mentioned previously, there is an important point to bear in mind when using numbers instead of a string label, such as coding male as 1 rather than m and female as 2 rather than f. When numbers are used like this, their magnitude has no correspondence with that of the feature they represent: the numbers are merely acting as labels or names. This is known technically as a nominal scale.

The danger is that you may forget that in a nominal scale the size of the numbers has no meaning. Once you have numbers, you can apply arithmetic and statistical operations to them even if they are not appropriate. For example, if you have coded sex of respondents as 2 for male and 1 for female, you can calculate the mean 'score' on the sex factor. If you have an equal number of men and women your mean 'score' will be 1.5. But this is nonsense: 1.5 does not mean anything at all. A mistake like this occurs when the researcher forgets that the numbers for this variable are only a nominal scale, and wrongly applies to the numbers procedures that are only relevant to more sophisticated types of scale where the magnitude of the numbers does reflect the size of the variable. (These are known as interval scales and ratio scales.)

24.3 Know what you want to find out

SPSS/PC+ provides the opportunity to carry out a wide range of statistical procedures very rapidly and with little effort. The danger is that because it offers such power, the researcher is tempted to comb the data: *"Let's do a factor analysis / multiple regression / 100 t-tests... and see what happens."*

It must be emphasised that there are real dangers in this approach. First, there is the statistical problem of interpreting significance levels when you have done a series of significance tests after the data has been given a preliminary examination. Practically, there is a risk of obtaining masses of analyses which overwhelm your ability to interpret and understand them: faced with a 4-inch pile of listing paper, many researchers, after the first flush of enthusiasm, have regretted their unrestrained proliferation of analyses!

Decide before you get to the computer what you want to find out, what statistical analyses you wish to apply. The power of the program is not a substitute for clear thinking. Without a definite idea of what you are looking for and how to find it you are likely to generate confusion rather than understanding.

25

Transferring Files between SPSS/PC+ and other Programs

25.1 Transferring the output file to a word processor

The .lis files created by SPSS/PC+ can be readily imported into a word processing package. With MS Word, for example, you simply uses the normal Transfer Load procedure and, when asked which file to load, type in the name of the .lis file, such as ex1.lis. The .lis file is formatted with an 80-column line, so many of the lines wrap over, but it is quite straightforward to remove lines or shorten them by deleting characters so that the .lis file takes on a neat appearance. When first loaded, the .lis file has bold character formatting which can be turned off using the normal commands of the word processor. Once the editing has been done, the file can be saved in the normal way as a document file.

25.2 Inputting data from other packages

With so many packages in use, it is impossible to give precise instructions here, but it is possible to import files from some other computer packages into SPSS/PC+, using the TRANSLATE FROM command. The manual describes how to do this for 1-2-3, Symphony and dBase files. Other packages may contain their own instructions on how their files can be imported. For example, EPIINFO is a package used for keeping medical records, and contains a procedure for converting files into a form that allows them to be imported into SPSS/PC+.

25.3 Importing a command file

You can write the data and command files on a word processor, and then load them into SPSS/PC+ to run them and carry out the data analysis. When using a word processor, each line of data or commands must be ended with a carriage-return, and the file must be saved as an ASCII (non-document) file. (A more detailed explanation is provided in the SPSS/PC+ manual.) To load the file into SPSS/PC+, use the normal F3 *Edit different file* procedure, and type in the name of the file when invited to do so.

26

Conclusion

26.1 Seeing what your SPSS/PC+ installation contains

To find out what SPSS/PC+ programs are installed on you computer, select *session control and info* from the main menu, go right and select *SPSS MANAGER,* go right and select *STATUS*. Press (R) and the whole command SPSS MANAGER STATUS will be pasted into the scratchpad. Running this command will provide a list of the SPSS/PC+ procedures installed.

26.2 Concluding comment

You have now reached the end of this introduction to SPSS/PC+. The book set out with the aim of teaching you how to use the package, and to demonstrate most of the facilities available in the Base module. Some of the procedures have not been covered; for example, WRITE writes cases to an ASCII file, AGGREGATE creates a .SYS file and aggregates groups of cases into a single case and WEIGHT adjusts the weighting of cases for an analysis (the default is 1.00). (All the procedures and commands are, of course, described very fully in the manuals.) In addition, there has been no attempt to explain all the menu and submenu entries: there are literally hundreds, many of which are likely to be used very rarely.

In this book, one short set of data has been used to demonstrate how to achieve the statistical analyses available in SPSS/PC+. The principles apply to any set of data, so you should have little difficulty in generalising your skill to your own sets of data. Remember to describe the layout of the data file in the DATA LIST line, and to be consistent in the use of variable names throughout the command file.

With the experience you now have of the way the package is driven, you should be able to investigate the additional facilities not covered in this book comparatively easily. Furthermore, you should now be able to approach the SPSS/PC+ Manuals with more understanding than before. The manuals are not very helpful for the complete beginner, but now that you know how commands operate, the file structure used by the package, and how to inspect the output, you should be able to make sense of (most of) them, assuming you understand the statistical procedures a particular command invokes.

Although SPSS/PC+ can be daunting when you first come across it, and can appear laborious in operation until you are familiar with its conventions, it does provide an enormously powerful tool. You may find that the Base module does not contain the procedures needed for your specific data analysis problem, but once you have mastered the Base module, you can face the Optional modules, such as Advanced Statistics with understanding of the principles upon which SPSS/PC+ works.

27

When things go wrong: Faced with the Unexpected

When learning how to use SPSS/PC+, there will certainly be occasions when the package does not operate as you expected or intended. Some of the more common problems, and how to correct them, are listed here.

Pressing (R) when the cursor is on the last line of a file does not move it down to an empty line, and it stays on the last line of the file which scrolls up the screen.

Create a new empty line below the last line of the file by pressing F4 and select Insert after *(R)*

Decimals in the data are not read

Ensure the DATA LIST line specifies the number of decimals in the scores on the particular variable e.g. sales 20-27 (2) is used to indicate that the data on sales is in columns 20-27 and has two decimal places such as: 11111.11

End of the line is reached when typing into a typing window

Press (R) to paste the contents of the typing window into the scratchpad, and use Alt T to get another typing window. Type in the rest of the material you want inserted into the file. See Section 9.3

F9 will not operate

If you have chosen zoom *so that the whole screen is filled with the .lis file, you must unzoom with Esc before the file can be saved. See Section 11.5*

File not found is shown when you try to load a file from DOS

See Section 3.8

Menus disappear

Restore the menus with Alt M

Not found is shown when you try to type in from the keyboard

Switch to edit mode and try again. See Section 5.5

Not available in menu mode is shown when you press a Function key

Switch to edit mode with Alt E and try again

Output shows more lines of data than you have cases

The data file contains empty line(s). Edit the data file to remove them. See Section 10.2

Pressing the wrong Function key

Press Esc. See Section 5.8

SPSS/PC: is the only thing shown on the screen

You have exited to the system prompt. Type review. *and press F10 and (R) to return to Review. See Section 5.11*

Unsaved changes ok to exit? n **is shown when you try to invoke SPSS/PC+ (with F10) or when you try to retrieve a different file**

You have made some changes to the file in the scratchpad and have not saved the altered version. If you need to save the contents of the scratchpad, press (R) and then save the file before pressing F10 or F3 again. If you do not want to save the scratchpad, type y *(R). See Section 9.4*

You set an anlysis running but want to stop it.

When the program is carrying out an analysis, it can be stopped by pressing Ctrl Break.

You want the output to run on, not stopping and showing MORE.

To turn off the routine that pauses the screen display of the output, insert the following command into the command file:

SET /MORE OFF.

This can be typed in, or can be created from the menus by selecting *session control & info*, then selecting *SET,* then *operations.*

28

Summary of the Menu Structure

This summary only shows a small section of the menu system of SPSS/PC+ which goes to at least six levels, and contains hundreds of entries, so that a complete map would be unwieldy. Once you are familiar with the system you can explore the various entries at the different levels.

In the menus, a word in CAPITALS is a command you can paste into the scratchpad by putting the cursor over it and pressing (R). If an entry is preceded by !, it is a compulsory component of that command. When using ANOVA, for example, the command line must include /VARIABLES and the variables must be specified by name. A menu entry in lower case letters cannot be pasted into the scratchpad by pressing (R); they may lead to submenus. When items have to be typed in, a typing window may be presented automatically or you can obtain a typing-in window with Alt T and then key in the details needed.

The main commands mentioned in the text are shown in the left-hand column, in alphabetical order. The second column shown the main menu entry and submenu entries to select to reach the submenu that contains the command shown in the left-hand column. The right hand column shows the more important entries in the submenu below the entry in the left-hand column. So, for example, to find the command COMPUTE from the main menu top level, select the *modify data or files* entry; from the submenu then revealed, select the *modify data values* entry. COMPUTE will be in the submenu then shown. If you move the menu cursor so it is over COMPUTE and press the right-arrow key, another submenu will be revealed, and it contains (among other items) *!target, !=* and *!instructions*. The presence of useful items in the next sublevel down is shown by :

PROCEDURE COMMAND	ROUTE FROM TOP LEVEL OF MAIN MENU	SUBMENU'S MAIN CONTENTS
AGGREGATE	modify data or files manipulate files	!/OUTFILE --- !/BREAK --- !aggregate variables
ANOVA	analyze data comparing group means	!/VARIABLES --- /OPTIONS --- /STATISTICS ---
AUTORECODE	modify data or files modify data values	!/VARIABLES !/INTO
CHISQUARE (one-sample)	analyze data other NPAR TESTS	!variable list
COMPUTE	modify data or files modify data values	!target != !instructions ---
CORRELATIONS	analyze data correlation & regression	!/VARIABLES --- /STATISTICS ---
COUNT	modify data or files modify data values	!target != !variables !() ---
CROSSTABS	analyze data descriptive statistics	!/TABLES --- /OPTIONS --- /STATISTICS ---
DATA LIST	read or write data	FILE" FIXED/ ---
DESCRIPTIVES	analyze data descriptive statistics	!/VARIABLES /OPTIONS --- /STATISTICS ---
DOS	run DOS or other pgms	

EXAMINE	analyze data descriptive statistics	!/VARIABLES --- /PLOT --- /STATISTICS ---
FINISH		
FLIP	modify data or files manipulate files	/VARIABLES
FREQUENCIES	analyze data descriptive statistics	!/VARIABLES /FORMAT --- /BARCHART --- /HISTOGRAM --- /PERCENTILES /STATISTICS ---
FRIEDMAN	analyze data other NPAR TESTS	!variable list
GET	read or write data	!/FILE" /DROP
IF	modify data or files modify data values	!condition --- !target != !instructions ---
JOIN ADD	modify data or files manipulate files	!/FILE ---
JOIN MATCH	modify data or files manipulate files	!/FILE ---
KRUSKAL-WALLIS	analyze data other NPAR TESTS	!variable list !BY !grouping variable
LIST	analyze data reports and tables	/VARIABLES /CASES ---
MANN-WHITNEY	analyze data other NPAR TESTS	!test variable !BY !grouping variable

MEANS	analyze data descriptive statistics	!/TABLES --- /OPTIONS --- /STATISTICS ---
MISSING VALUE	read or write data labels and formatting	!variables ()
MODIFY VARS	read or write data	/RENAME ---
N	modify data or files select or weight data	!n of cases
ONEWAY	analyze data comparing group means	!/VARIABLES --- /RANGES --- /OPTIONS --- /STATISTICS ---
PLOT	graph data	/FORMAT --- /TITLE" /VERTICAL --- /HORIZONTAL --- /VSIZE /HSIZE !/PLOT ---
PROCESS IF	modify data or files select or weight data	!() ---
RANK	modify data or files modify data values	!variables order --- BY ranking functions ---
RECODE	modify data or files modify data values	!variables () ---
REGRESSION	analyze data correlation & regression	!/VARIABLES --- /DESCRIPTIVES --- !/DEPENDENT !/METHOD --- residual analysis ---

REPORT	analyze data reports and tables	/FORMAT --- !/VARIABLES --- /TITLE --- /BREAK --- /SUMMARY --- /OUTFILE"
SAMPLE	modify data or files select or weight data	sampling fraction FROM
SAVE	read or write data	/OUTFILE"
SELECT IF	modify data or files select or weight data	!() ---
SET	session control and info	output --- operations ---
SORT	modify data or files manipulate files	sort variable(s) (A) (D)
SPSS MANAGER	session control and info	STATUS
SUBTITLE"	session control and info titles and comments	
TITLE"	session control and info titles and comments	
T-TEST	analyze data comparing group means	/GROUPS --- /VARIABLES /PAIRS ---
VALUE LABELS	read or write data labels and formatting	!variables !value "
VARIABLE LABELS	read or write data labels and formatting	!variables !"
WILCOXON	analyze data other NPAR TESTS	!variable list

WRITE   read or write data   /VARIABLES
                                                           /CASES

YRMODA   modify data or files
                         modify data values
                         IF
                         !instructions
                         functions

Appendix A

Answers to Exercises

Exercise 10.1

```
TITLE 'Alcohol intake study'.
DATA LIST FILE 'a:alcdat' FIXED /id 1-4 age 6-7 sex 9 alcint 11.
VARIABLE LABELS alcint 'Alcohol intake per week'.
VALUE LABELS sex 1 'male' 2 'female'/alcint 1 'none' 2 'low' 3 'medium' 4
'high'.
MISSING VALUE age(-1) sex(-1) alcint(-1).
SET /LISTING 'a:alc.lis'.
FREQUENCIES /VARIABLES alcint.
```

One can have different names for the variables. Providing the variable names are used consistently throughout the file, and the file contains the lines shown, it would be successful.

Exercise 13.1

```
GET /FILE 'a:ex1.sys'.
SET /LISTING 'a:ex3.lis'.
EXAMINE /VARIABLES cust.
EXAMINE /VARIABLES cust BY area /FREQUENCIES FROM (20) BY (10).
EXAMINE /VARIABLES area /PLOT HISTOGRAM.
```

The first procedure, EXAMINE /VARIABLES cust., produces the output shown in Fig 13.1. The second EXAMINE procedure gives summary statistics and a stem-leaf plot for the whole set of data (thus repeating the output of the first EXAMINE command) and then the scores on cust for each area separately, as shown in Fig A1.1. The subcommand /FREQUENCIES..., following the BY area instruction, yields tables such as shown in Fig 13.3 for each area. (These are not shown in Fig A1.1.) Observe in Fig A1.1 that this EXAMINE command gives separate box-plots, on one graph, for each area. (The meaning of box-plots is described in section 21.4.)

The final EXAMINE command produces summary statistics and a simple histogram of the frequency of scores which can be seen at the end of Fig A1.1. The histogram gives the frequency, the number of cases in each score interval, and plots the appropriate number of asterisks. But the central value of each interval, referred to in the printout as '*bin center*', which should be 1 and 2 since these are the two values of the variable area, are printed as 2 and 3.

Another aspect of Fig A1.1 deserves mention, and illustrates the point made in section 13.5. The final command line produces summary statistics on area, which is a nominal variable: the two areas of the country are coded as 1 or 2, but the magnitude of the numbers is meaningless, they are simply used as labels. The printout shows the mean of the area variable to be 1.5909: as stated in section 13.5, this is nonsensical, and the investigator needs to examine the printout carefully to ensure there is no misinterpretation of the numbers.

```
EXAMINE /VARIABLES cust BY area /FREQUENCIES FROM (20) BY (10) .

        CUST
By      AREA            1               north

Valid cases:            9.0     Missing cases:      .0      Percent missing:    .0

Mean      51.2222  Std Err   6.1639   Min     30.0000  Skewness 1.0009
Median    43.0000  Varian  341.9444   Max     83.0000  S E Skew   .7171
5% Trim   50.6358  Std Dev  18.4917   Range   53.0000  Kurtosis -.2788
                                      IQR     29.0000  S E Kurt  1.3997
```

```
        CUST
By      AREA            1               north

Frequency   Stem &  Leaf
   2.00       3   .  09
   4.00       4   .  0138
   1.00       5   .  8
    .00       6   .
   1.00       7   .  9
   1.00       8   .  3

Stem width:10
Each leaf:1 case(s)
```

```
        CUST
By      AREA        2            south

Valid cases:13.0  Missing cases:      .0      Percent missing:    .0

Mean      50.5385  Std Err  4.6266  Min      28.0000  Skewness  .3601
Median    46.0000  Varian  278.2692 Max      76.0000  S E Skew   .6163
5% Trim   50.3761  Std Dev 16.6814  Range    48.0000  Kurtosis -1.5159
                                    IQR      32.5000  S E Kurt  1.1909
```

```
        CUST
By      AREA        2            south

Frequency   Stem  &  Leaf
    1.00      2    .  8
    4.00      3    .  3689
    3.00      4    .  268
     .00      5    .
    2.00      6    .  08
    3.00      7    .  126

Stem width:10
Each leaf:1 case(s)
```

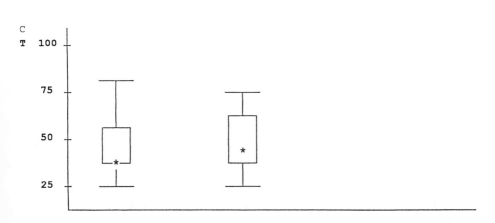

```
AREA              1                 2
N of Cases      9.00             13.00
Symbol Key:     * – Median       (O) – Outlier    (E) – Extreme
```

```
EXAMINE /VARIABLES area /PLOT HISTOGRAM.
      AREA
```

Valid cases:	22.0	Missing cases:	.0	Percent missing: .0

Mean	1.5909	Std Err	.1073	Min	1.0000	Skewness	−.3974
Median	2.0000	Variance	.2532	Max	2.0000	S E Skew	.4910
5% Trim	1.6010	Std Dev	.5032	Range	1.0000	Kurtosis	−2.0367
				IQR	1.0000	S E Kurt	.9528

Frequency	Bin Center	
9.00	2	*********
13.00	3	*************

```
Bin width : 1
Each star: 1 case(s)
```

Fig A1.1 Extract of the ouput from the Exercise 13.1 command file.

Exercise 14.1

```
GET /FILE 'a:ex1.sys'.
SET /LISTING 'a:ex4.lis'.
FREQUENCIES /VARIABLES sex employer.
FREQUENCIES /VARIABLES employer /FORMAT DVALUE.
FREQUENCIES /VARIABLES cust /FORMAT NOTABLE /STATISTICS ALL.
DESCRIPTIVES /VARIABLES cust /STATISTICS ALL.
```

The first FREQUENCIES command produces a simple table showing the number of cases with each score on the the variable named, as shown in Fig 10.3. The second FREQUENCIES line illustrates the /FORMAT DVALUE subcommand. As Fig A1.2 shows, the effect is to have the values of the variable (employer in this example) given in descending order.

The last FREQUENCIES command does not provide a table of frequencies, because the /FORMAT NOTABLE subcommand suppresses it. The /STATISTICS ALL gives the summary statistics shown in Fig A1.2. The DESCRIPTIVES... /STATISTICS ALL line produces a similar table of summary statistics, as can be seen in Fig A1.2, except that it does not include the mode and median values which FREQUENCIES.../STATISTICS ALL gives.

FREQUENCIES /VARIABLES employer /FORMAT DVALUE.
EMPLOYER

Value Label	Value	Frequency	Percent	Valid Percent	Cum Percent
	3	6	27.3	27.3	27.3
	2	8	36.4	36.4	63.6
	1	8	36.4	36.4	100.0
	TOTAL	22	100.0	100.0	
Valid Cases 22		Missing Cases	0		

FREQUENCIES /VARIABLES cust /FORMAT NOTABLE /STATISTICS ALL.

CUST   customers visited

Mean	50.818	Std Err	3.627	Median	44.500
Mode	39.000	Std Dev	17.012	Variance	289.394
Kurtosis	-1.000	S E Kurt	.953	Skewness	.605
S E Skew	.491	Range	55.000	Minimum	28.000
Maximum	83.000	Sum	1118.000		

Valid Cases 22   Missing Cases 0

DESCRIPTIVES /VARIABLES cust /STATISTICS ALL.

Number of Valid Observations (Listwise) =   22.00

Variable CUST   customers visited

Mean	50.818	S.E. Mean	3.627
Std Dev	17.012	Variance	289.394
Kurtosis	-1.000	S.E. Kurt	.953
Skewness	.605	S.E. Skew	.491
Range	55.000	Minimum	28
Maximum	83	Sum	1118.000

Valid Observations 22   Missing Observations   0

Fig A1.2. Extract of the output from the Exercise 14.1 command file

Exercise 14.2

```
GET /FILE 'a:exl.sys'.
SET /LISTING 'a:ex5.lis'.
CROSSTABS /TABLES area BY employer /OPTIONS 5.
CROSSTABS /TABLES sex BY employer /STATISTICS 1.
CROSSTABS /TABLES sex BY employer BY area.
```

The output is shown in Fig A1.3. The first CROSSTABS line gives a table showing the number of cases from each area/employer, and the /OPTIONS 5 subcommand gives each frequency expressed as a percentage of the total number of cases.

The second CROSSTABS produces a table similar to Fig 14.2, but employer forms the columns and sex forms the rows; this shows how easy it is to have the table rotated simply be choosing the appropriate order of naming the variables in the /TABLES... section of the command line. The /STATISTICS 1 subcommand gives a chi-square test, although it is not valid as the printout shows that 6 of 6 cells in the table have an Expected frequency (E.F.) of less than 5.

The last CROSSTABS demonstrates the use of a control variable: separate sex by employer tables are given for each value of area.

```
CROSSTABS /TABLES AREA BY EMPLOYER /OPTIONS 5.
```

Crosstabulation: AREA
                    By EMPLOYER

EMPLOYER->	Count Tot Pct	1	2	3	Row Total
AREA					
1 north	1	5	1	3	9
		22.7	4.5	13.6	40.9
2 south	2	3	7	3	13
		13.6	31.8	13.6	59.1
	Column Total	8	8	6	22
		36.4	36.4	27.3	100.0

Number of Missing Observations =0

CROSSTABS /TABLES SEX BY EMPLOYER /STATISTICS 1.

Crosstabulation: SEX
                  By EMPLOYER

EMPLOYER->	Count				Row
		1	2	3	Total
SEX					
1 male		4	3	3	10 47.6
2 female		4	4	3	11 52.4
	Column Total	8 38.1	7 33.3	6 28.6	21 100.0

Chi-Square	D.F.	Significance	Min E.F.	Cells with E.F.< 5
.09545	2	.9534	2.857	6 OF 6 (100.0%)

Number of Missing Observations =1

CROSSTABS /TABLES SEX BY EMPLOYER BY AREA.

Crosstabulation: SEX
                  By EMPLOYER
   Controlling for AREA
                                                    = 1 north

EMPLOYER->	Count				Row
		1	2	3	Total
SEX					
1 male		2	1		3 33.3
2 female		3	1	2	6 66.7
	Column Total	5 55.6	1 11.1	3 33.3	9 100.0

```
Crosstabulation:  SEX
                  By EMPLOYER
                  Controlling for AREA
                                                        = 2 south
```

EMPLOYER->	Count				Row
		1	2	3	Total
SEX					
	1	2	3	2	7
male					58.3
	2	1	3	1	5
female					41.7
	Column	3	6	3	12
	Total	25.0	50.0	25.0	100.0

Number of Missing Observations =1

Fig A1.3 Output from the Exercise 14.2 command file.

Exercise 15.1

```
GET /FILE 'a:ex1.sys'.
SET /LISTING 'a:ex6.lis'.
MEANS /TABLES sales BY sex area.
MEANS /TABLES sales BY sex /OPTIONS 6 8 12.
```

The first MEANS command produces tables showing the mean scores on sales for each level of sex (the same table as Fig 15.1) and then a similar table for each level of area. The second MEANS command demonstrates the use of the /OPTIONS subcommand: the output is shown in Fig A1.4. With options 6 and 12, the table includes the sum and variance for each group. Option 8 is included to suppress the printing of value labels; without it, the command will fail. The *missing case* mentioned in the printout is the respondent whose sex was recorded in the original data file as 3, indicating that their sex was not known.

```
MEANS /TABLES sales BY sex /OPTIONS 6 8 12.
```

```
Summaries of        SALES
By levels of        SEX
```

Variable	Value	Sum	Mean	Std Dev	Variance	Cases
Population:		122470.330	5831.9205	2377.9699	5654740.79	21
SEX	1	59506.3700	5950.6370	2772.4555	7686509.34	10
SEX	2	62963.9600	5723.9964	2089.1906	4364717.18	11

```
Total Cases =       22
```

```
Missing Cases =     1 OR 4.5 PCT.
```

Fig A1.4 Extract of output from the Exercise 15.1 command file

Exercise 18.1

```
GET /FILE 'a:ex1.sys'.
SET /LISTING 'a:ex9.lis'.
NPAR TESTS /MANN-WHITNEY sales BY sex(1,2).
RANK cust sales.
CORRELATIONS /VARIABLES rcust rsales.
RANK cust BY employer /RANK INTO rnkbyem.
SORT employer.
LIST id employer rnkbyem.
```

The NPAR line produces an output similar to Fig 18.4, but comparing `sales` by `sex` rather than by `employer`.

The output from the other commands is given in Fig A1.5. The RANK command produces two new variables, `rcust` and `rsales`, which are the ranked values of `cust` and `sales` as the printout indicates. The CORRELATIONS yields the rank correlation between `cust` and `sales` as it calculates the correlation between `rcust` and `rsales`. In this instance the correlation is .8153, and the two asterisks indicate this is significant at the .001 level.

The second RANK command illsutrates the use of the /RANK INTO subcommand. The scores on the variable `cust` are ranked for each employer separately, as a result of the RANK cust BY employer instruction, and the name of the new variable created by this ranking procedure is defined as `rnkbyem` (standing for 'rank-by-employer').

In order to obtain a clearer printout of these `rnkbyem` values, the SORT command is used to have the data sorted according to employer, and the data is then printed out using the LIST command. As can be seen in Fig A1.5, the data for respondents from employer 1 are all listed, then the data for respondents from employer 2 and finally the data for respondents from employer 3.

The column of `rnkbyem` values in Fig A1.5 shows how the RANK cust BY employer instruction operated: the 8 respondents from employer 1 were ranked from 1 to 8, the 8 respondents from employer 2 were ranked from 1 to 8, and the 6 respondents from employer 3 were ranked from 1 to 6. Some of the `rnkbyem` values are not whole numbers (e.g. in the employer 1 set, two scores are 7.5000); this is because when two respondents had the same score on `cust`, they were given the mean value of the ranks appropriate to their scores. For example, the two largest scores on `cust` for respondents from employer 1 were both 48, corresponding to rank values of 7 and 8; so both these scores are assigned a rank of 7.5.

```
RANK cust sales.

From            New
variable        variable      Label

CUST            RCUST         RANK of CUST
SALES           RSALES        RANK of SALES
```

```
CORRELATIONS /VARIABLES rcust rsales.

Correlations:  RCUST          RSALES
RCUST          1.0000         .8153**
RSALES         .8153**        1.0000

N of cases:        22                  1-tailed Signif:* - .01** - .001

'' . '' is printed if a coefficient cannot be computed
```

```
RANK cust BY employer /RANK INTO rnkbyem.

From            New
variable        variable      Label

CUST            RNKBYEM       RANK of CUST by EMPLOYER

SORT employer.
```

```
LIST id employer rnkbyem.
```

ID	EMPLOYER	RNKBYEM
1	1	6.000
3	1	7.500
7	1	5.000
9	1	4.000
12	1	1.000
17	1	2.000
18	1	7.500
22	1	3.000
2	2	6.000
5	2	8.000
8	2	1.000
11	2	4.500
14	2	2.000
15	2	3.000
20	2	7.000
21	2	4.500
4	3	6.000
6	3	3.000
10	3	4.000
13	3	2.000
16	3	5.000
19	3	1.000

Number of cases read = 22 Number of cases listed = 22

Fig A1.5 Extract of the output from the Exercise 18.1 command file.

Exercise 19.1

```
SET /FILE 'a:ex1.sys'.
SET /LISTING 'a:ex11.lis'.
RECODE sales (7000 THRU HI = 2) (LO THRU 7000 = 1).
LIST id sales.
```

The output from this command file is shown in Fig A1.6.

```
RECODE sales (7000 THRU HI = 2) (LO THRU 7000 = 1) .
LIST id sales.
```

ID	SALES
1	1.00
2	1.00
3	2.00
4	2.00
5	1.00
6	1.00
7	1.00
8	1.00
9	1.00
10	2.00
11	1.00
12	1.00
13	2.00
14	1.00
15	1.00
16	2.00
17	1.00
18	2.00
19	2.00
20	1.00
21	1.00
22	1.00

Number of cases read =22 Number of cases listed = 22

Fig A1.6 Output from the Exercise 19.1 command file

One may wish to confirm that the RECODE has operated as one expected, and list both the original scores and the recoded ones. Once the scores have been recoded, the original scores are lost from the Active File, and so cannot be listed. The way round this is to COMPUTE a new variable, which is simply a copy of the original scores before the RECODE is carried out. The recoding will not, of course, affect the new variable, and so one retains in the Active File both the original scores and the recoded ones. The command file shown in Fig A1.7 shows how this is achieved. A new variable, osales, is computed by the COMPUTE line. The sales data is then RECODEd, and both osales and the recoded sales are LISTed. The listing (Fig A1.7) shows that the original sales figures from 7000 upward have been recoded as 2, lower values being recoded as 1.

```
COMPUTE osales = sales.
RECODE sales (7000 thru hi = 2) (lo thru 7000 = 1).
LIST id osales sales.
```

ID	OSALES	SALES
1	3450.60	1.00
2	4984.42	1.00
3	10432.82	2.00
4	8235.21	2.00
5	6441.38	1.00
6	6497.05	1.00
7	3835.26	1.00
8	3819.00	1.00
9	5723.52	1.00
10	7937.45	2.00
11	4582.44	1.00
12	2005.30	1.00
13	8914.50	2.00
14	3124.20	1.00
15	4222.45	1.00
16	8881.28	2.00
17	3449.35	1.00
18	7882.60	2.00
19	8779.00	2.00
20	5822.68	1.00
21	4004.80	1.00
22	5886.40	1.00

Number of cases read = 22 Number of cases listed = 22

Fig A1.7 A command file and output that RECODEs and retains original scores.

Exercise 19.2

```
GET /FILE 'a:ex1.sys'.
SET /LISTING 'a:ex12.lis'.
COMPUTE newv1 = (att1 + att2).
LIST id att1 att2 newv1.
```

In this command file the LIST instruction asks for a listing of the respondent's id and the original att1 and att2 scores as well as newv1, the sum of att1 and att2. The output, shown in Fig A1.8, allows one to check that the program has calculated newv1 in the way one intended.

ID	ATT1	ATT2	NEWV1
1	4	5	9.00
2	4	4	8.00
3	2	3	5.00
4	2	3	5.00
5	2	2	4.00
6	3	3	6.00
7	3	2	5.00
8	4	5	9.00
9	2	3	5.00
10	1	2	3.00
11	2	3	5.00
12	2	3	5.00
13	2	2	4.00
14	1	2	3.00
15	5	4	9.00
16	2	2	4.00
17	3	4	7.00
18	2	3	5.00
19	4	3	7.00
20	1	3	4.00
21	3	4	7.00
22	2	3	5.00

Number of cases read = 22 Number of cases listed = 22

Fig A1.8 Output from the command file for Exercise 19.2.

Exercise 20.1

```
GET /FILE 'a:ex1.sys'.
SET /LISTING 'a:ex13.lis'.
PROCESS IF (att1 = 1).
DESCRIPTIVES /VARIABLES att3.
PROCESS IF (area = 2).
FREQUENCIES /VARIABLES att2.
```

The output is shown in Fig A1.9. The first table shows the mean, standard deviation, minimum and maximum of scores on att3 for those respondents who scored 1 on att1 (selected by the first PROCESS IF command).

The second table shows the scores on att2 for those respondents who had a score of 2 on the variable area. Note the use of PROCESS IF, not SELECT IF, to achieve this outcome.

```
PROCESS IF (att1=1).
DESCRIPTIVES /VARIABLES att3.
```

Number of Valid Observations (Listwise) = 3.00

Variable	Mean	Std Dev	Minimum	Maximum	N Label
ATT3	4.33	.58	4	5	3

```
PROCESS IF (area=2).
```

```
FREQUENCIES /VARIABLES att2.
```

ATT2

Value Label	Value	Frequency	Percent	Valid Cum Percent	Percent
	2	5	38.5	38.5	38.5
	3	3	23.1	23.1	61.5
	4	4	30.8	30.8	92.3
	5	1	7.7	7.7	100.0
	TOTAL	13	100.0	100.0	

Valid Cases   13   Missing Cases   0

Fig A1.9 Output from the Exercise 20.1 command file

Appendix B

The Basics of Statistical Analysis

Contents of this appendix are as follows:

B6 Statistical significance and testing hypotheses
B6.1 The concept of statistical significance
B6.2 Significance level
B6.3 Type I and type II errors
B6.4 One and two-tailed hypotheses

B7 Parametric and non-parametric tests

B8 Analyzing nominal data: Chi-square
B8.1 The two-way chi-square
B8.2 The one-sample chi-square
B8.3 Essential requirements for the chi-square test

B9 Parametric tests
B9.1 The t-test
    B9.1.1 The independent t-test
    B9.1.2 The related, paired or within-subjects t-test
B9.2 Analysis of Variance
    B9.2.1 Basic concepts
    B9.2.2 Obtaining one-way anovar
    B9.2.3 Two-way anovar
    B9.2.4 Range tests

B10 Correlation
B10.1 The concept of correlation
B10.2 Parametric correlation: Pearson product moment correlation
B10.3 Non-parametric correlation: Spearman Rank (rho)
B10.4 Regression
B10.5 Multiple regression

B11 Nonparametric tests
B11.1 Deciding which test to use
B11.2 Wilcoxon test
B11.3 Friedman test
B11.4 Mann-Whitney test
B11.5 Kruskal-Wallis test

B12 Interpreting the outcome of a significance test

Introduction

The main body of this book assumes that the user knows the statistical analyses that are needed, and describes the procedures for getting SPSS/PC+ to provide particular statistics and apply specific statistical tests. The aim of this appendix is to remind readers of the principles of statistical analysis, so that they can decide which statistics they need for their particular sets of data. It is not intended as a substitute for a text on statistics, but should be seen rather as an aide-memoire for those who have temporarily forgotten what the various statistical procedures are used for.

B1 Fundamental definitions

B1.1 Population and sample

A population is an entire set of objects or people, such as the residents of France or Australian nine-year olds. A sample is a subset of a population, and in the majority of research analysis one works with a sample of a population. Usually one hopes to generalize from the sample to the population, as in opinion polls where perhaps 1,000 people are asked for their opinion, the results obtained from this sample are generalized to the whole voting population of the country, and statements are made about the popularity of political parties in the country as a whole.

Whether it is valid to generalize from the sample to the population depends upon the size of the sample and whether it is representative of the population: does it have the same characteristics as the population of which it is a subset?

B1.2 Descriptive and inferential statistics

Descriptive statistics are used to describe and summarize sets of data. They answer questions such as "What was the average age of the patients who were admitted to the local hospital with a heart attack in the last six months?"

Inferential statistics are used in generalizing from a sample to a wider population, and in testing hypotheses, deciding whether the data is consistent with the research prediction.

B1.3 Scales of measurement

B1.3.1

Nominal scales are where the numbers are used merely as a label. For example, we may code sex of respondent as 1 or 2, with 1 meaning male and 2 meaning female. The size of the numbers is meaningless, and 2 is not bigger or better than 1 (we could just as easily used 1 to indicate female and 2 to indicate male).

B1.3.2

In ordinal or rank scales there is some correspondence between the size of the numbers and the magnitude of the quality represented by the numbers. A common ordinal scale is position in a race. One knows that the person who came first (position 1) was faster than the person who came second (position 2), who was in turn faster than the person who came third (position 3). But the numbers 1, 2 and 3 do not tell you anything about the size of the differences between the three people. The winner, number 1, may have been well ahead of numbers 2 and 3, or number 1 may have just beaten number 2 with number three trailing far behind.

B1.3.3

With interval scales, the numbers do represent the magnitude of the differences. A frequently-cited example is the Celsius temperature scale, where the difference between 20 and 30 degrees is the same as the difference between 30 and 40 degrees. But note that the Celsius scale is not a ratio scale: something with a temperature of 40 degrees is not twice as hot as something with a temperature of 20 degrees.

B1.3.4

In ratio scales, there is a true zero point and the ratio of the numbers reflects the ratios of the attribute measured. For example, an object 30 cm long is twice the length of an object 15 cm long.

B1.4 Parametric and non-parametric data and tests

The distinction between types of scale is important as the type of scale determines which type of statistical analysis is appropriate. In order to use the parametric statistical tests, one should have used an interval or ratio scale of measurement. If the data is measured on an ordinal scale, one should use non-parametric tests. For nominal scales, some of the non-parametric tests, such as chi-square, are appropriate.

B1.5 Dependent and independent variables

In experiments, the experimenter manipulates the independent variable, and measures any consequential alterations in the dependent variable. If the experiment has been designed and carried out properly, it is assumed that the changes in the dependent variable are the results of the changes in the independent variable.

The distinction between dependent and independent variables is not restricted to research using the experimental method. When correlational studies are performed, one also has a dependent variable and independent variables. For example, there has been a considerable amount of research into the factors associated with students' success and failure at their courses. This research has correlated students' study habits and personality to their course grades; the grades form the dependent variable and the study habits and personality are independent variables.

B1.6 Within-subjects and between-subjects variables

If the same respondents are used in two or more conditions of an experiment, one has a within-subjects, or repeated-measures, design. When different respondents feature in the different conditions, one has a between-subjects, or independent groups, design. It is, of course, possible to combine the two into a mixed design. For example, one might have data on men and women's ability to drive when they have had no alcohol and when they have had a certain amount of alcohol. If one used the same subjects in the no-alcohol and the with-alcohol conditions, sex would be a between-subjects variable and alcohol would be a within-subjects variable.

Different statistical tests are appropriate for within-subjects and between-subjects variables, and it is important to ensure one is using the proper test for the data being analysed.

B2 Measures of central tendency: mode, median, mean

Given a set of scores or readings, one usually requires a single figure which indicates the 'typical' value of the set. There are three alternative figures one can use: mode, median and mean. Table B1 shows the scores of 22 respondents on an attitude-scale question, where the possible responses were coded as 1, 2, 3, 4 or 5 (it is taken from exdat, the file of data used in the main text of this book).

The MODE is the most frequently occurring value, in this instance 4.

The MEDIAN is the value that divides the distribution of scores in half: 50% of the scores fall below the median and 50% fall above it. When the scores are in ascending order, if there are an odd number of scores, the median is the middle score. If there are an even number of scores, average the two middle scores. In Table B1, there are 22 scores, so the median is obtained by taking the average of the 11th and 12th scores; in Table B1 these are both 4, so the median is 4.

Table B1. Scores on an attitude scale question

Respondent	Response
01	1
15	1
19	1
02	3
06	3
08	3
11	3
17	3
21	3
22	3
04	4
05	4
09	4
12	4
13	4
14	4
16	4
18	4
20	4
03	5
07	5
10	5

The arithmetic MEAN is obtained by totalling the scores and dividing the sum by the number of scores. In Table B1, the total of the scores is 75, and the mean is therefore $75/22 = 3.41$.

With SPSS/PC+, the mode can be obtained by using FREQUENCIES /VARIABLES variable-name /STATISTICS ALL.

The median is obtained from the EXAMINE procedure (see section 13.4) or with FREQUENCIES.../STATISTICS ALL (section 15.2).

There are a number of ways of obtaining the mean, including EXAMINE (section 13.4), FREQUENCIES... /STATISTICS (section 14.1), DESCRIPTIVES.../ STATISTICS (section 14.2). The means of subgroups are provided by the MEANS procedure (section 15.3). The output from parametric tests such as the T-TEST and ONEWAY procedures also include means of the subgroups being compared._

B3 Measures of Variability

B3.1 The concept of variability

An important feature of a set of data is the spread or variation of the scores in the set. We need to be able to express the variation within a set of scores as well as the central value (mode, median or mean) of the set. Table B2 shows the number of customers visited by male and female sales personnel (the figures are again taken from the exdat file used in the main text of this book).

Table B2. Customers visited by male and female personnel

Males		Females	
subject	n visits	subject	n visits
2:	46	1:	43
3:	48	6:	72
4:	83	7:	42
8:	28	11:	39
9:	41	14:	33
10:	76	15:	36
12:	30	16:	79
13:	68	18:	48
17:	38	19:	58
21:	39	20:	60
		22:	40

B3.2 Range; Interquartile range

The RANGE of a set of scores is simply the difference between the highest and lowest scores. So for the males in Table B2, the range is 83 – 28 = 55 and for females the range is 79 – 33 = 46. Range gives an indication of the spread of the scores, but of course it depends completely on just two figures from the whole set, the highest and the lowest. One very low or very high score will produce a large increase in the range, and this might be quite misleading.

One alternative measure is the Interquartile Range. As mentioned earlier, the MEDIAN is that score which divides the set into two halves, with half the scores falling below the median and half the scores falling above it. The median is the 50th percentile, which means 50% of the scores fall below it. We can also have a 25th percentile, which is the score below which 25% of the scores fall, a 75th percentile, a 90th percentile etc. The interquartile range is the difference between the 25th and 75th percentiles. The Interquartile Range for the two sets of data shown in Table B2 are 34 for males and 21 for females. The semi-interquartile range is the interquartile range divided by 2.

To obtain percentiles, the appropriate SPSS/PC+ command is FREQUENCIES /VARIABLES variable-name /PERCENTILES 25 50 75. The figures after the word PERCENTILES state the percentiles requested. If one uses FREQUENCIES /VARIABLES variable-name /NTILES 10, this requests every 10th percentile.

The range and Inter-Quartile range (IQR) are given if one uses the EXAMINE command (section 13.4).

Unlike the range, the interquartile range is not affected by a single score which is much greater or much less than the others. But it does use only two figures from the set to express the variability in the set, and so ignores most of the numbers.

B3.3 Variance and standard deviation

A better measure of variation would be one that used all the numbers in the set, not just two of them. This problem is tackled by looking at the mean of the set of scores, and taking the difference between each score and the mean. If one adds these deviations from the mean, the total is zero: so this figure is not going to be very helpful as an indication of the variation in the set of scores! The way round this is to square each of the deviations, which gets rid of all the negative numbers, and then add them up to obtain a sum of squared deviations. In order to get an idea of the variation in the set, it is sensible to take the average of the squared deviations. The sum of the squared deviations divided by n is known as the VARIANCE of the set of scores.

(Note: If you are using data from a sample as an estimate of a wider population, then divide by n-1 to obtain a better estimate of the population variance.)

The square root of the variance is the STANDARD DEVIATION, and is the number used to express the variation in the set of scores. The variance and standard deviation of a set of scores is found in SPSS/PC+ by EXAMINE (section 13.4), FREQUENCIES.../ STATISTICS (section 14.1) or DESCRIPTIVES.../ STATISTICS (section 14.2).

B4 Standard error and confidence limits

Inferential statistics involve estimating the characteristics of a population from the data obtained from a sample of that population. For example, one uses the mean of the sample to estimate the population mean. If one took a large set of samples from the population, the means of the samples would form a normal distribution. The standard deviation of that distribution is given by taking the standard deviation of the sample and dividing it by the square root of n, the number in the sample. This is the Standard Error, and it allows one to state the probability that the true mean of the population is within specified limits. From the properties of the normal distribution, it can be deduced that there is a 95% probability that the true mean of the population is within plus or minus approximately 2 standard errors of the sample mean. Suppose you have taken a sample of 100 subjects from a population and found that the mean of the sample is 50, and the standard deviation is 10. The standard error is 1.0 (10/square root of 100). One can conclude that the true mean of the population has a 95% probability of being within the limits 50 +or- (1 multiplied by 2) = 50 + or – 2 i.e. between 48 and 52.

So the 95% confidence interval means that there is a 95% probability that the true mean is between the limits specified. Confidence intervals are shown in printouts from the ONEWAY procedure, as shown in Fig 16.1.

B5 Frequency distributions

B5.1 Histograms and barcharts

A frequency distribution shows the number of times each score occurs in the set of scores under examination. Histograms and barcharts are graphical displays of the frequency distribution of the scores. Examples, obtained with the FREQUENCIES procedure in SPSS/PC+ are shown in Figs 21.1 and 21.2. In SPSS/PC+, a histogram shows values of the variable where there are no instances of that value being obtained (Fig 21.1), but these zero-frequency values are not shown in a barchart (Fig 21.2).

A frequency distribution can be symmetrical or skewed. If it is roughly symmetrical, the mean can be used as the measure of central tendency but if it is skewed the median should be used rather than the mean. A normal distribution, which is symmetrical, has a skewness statistic of zero. Kurtosis measures the extent to which observations are clustered in the tails; for a normal distribution, the kurtosis statistic is zero. SPSS/PC+ indicates the amount of skew and the kurtosis of a frequency distribution if one uses EXAMINE (section 13.4 and Fig 13.1), FREQUENCIES.../ STATISTICS ALL or DESCRIPTIVES.../STATISTICS ALL (see the output from Exercise 14.1 in chapter 29).

B5.2 The normal distribution curve

The normal distribution curve is fundamental to statistical analysis. It is a frequency distribution: if we take large sets of data for biological functions such as body height, the resulting frequency distribution is a normal curve.

The normal distribution curve is symmetrical, with the 'middle' being equal to the mean. One can measure off the horizontal axis in standard deviations from the mean. Very nearly all the distribution lies between −3sd and +3sd from the mean. Tables of the normal curve, found in most statistics texts, give the proportion of the curve falling above and below any position on the horizontal axis. From such tables, it is easy to find the proportion of the curve between any two points on the horizontal axis.

B5.3 z scores

When a series of parametric data is transformed so that it has a mean of zero and a standard deviation of 1.00, the scores are known as z-scores. To obtain the z-scores of a set of data, use the command DESCRIPTIVES /VARIABLES variable-name /OPTIONS 3.

B6 Statistical significance and testing hypotheses

B6.1 Statistical significance

The data in Table B3, taken from the exdat file used in the main part of this book, shows the number of customers visited by the sales personnel of two employers (labelled 2 and 3).

Table B3 Customer visits by sales personnel from two employers

Employer 2		Employer 3	
subject	n visits	subject	n visits
2:	46	4:	83
5:	71	6:	72
8:	28	10:	76
11:	39	13:	68
14:	33	16:	79
15:	36	19:	58
20:	60		
21:	39		
Mean: 44.00		Mean: 72.67	

The question that the researcher asks is: is there a statistically significant difference between the means of the scores of the two groups of sales personnel?

In Table B3, group 2 has the smaller mean, and so you might wish to conclude that these people made fewer visits. But look at subject 5 in group 2 and subject 19 in group 3: the group 3 member has a smaller score than the group 2 member. So if you took just those two subjects, you could not say that group 2 had the lower score.

If there were no difference between the two groups, their mean scores would be the 'same'. This does not imply, of course, that they would be identical, because responses almost always show some variance (variability). This random, unexplained variation is due to chance. For example, the variation in the scores for group 2 in Table B3 is variation due to chance. The mean for subjects 2, 5, 8 and 11 in group 2 is 46 and the mean for subjects 14, 15, 20 and 21 from the same group is 42. The difference between these two means is simply due to chance, random variation. It arises even though both these subgroups come from one 'population' (the complete set of scores given by group 2 subjects).

Our question now is: is the difference between the means of group 2 and group 3 also simply due to chance?

If the difference between the means of group 2 and group 3 is due to chance, then groups 2 and 3 are samples from the same 'population', just as subjects 2-11 and 14-21 of group 2 are samples from one population.

To decide whether groups 2 and 3 are samples from one population or are 'really' different and come from different populations, one applies a test of statistical significance. The significance tests let you estimate how likely it is that the data from the separate groups of subjects come from one population. If it is unlikely that they came from the same population, you can conclude that they didn't, and that they came from separate populations.

In significance testing we look at the difference between the scores and compare it with the amount of variation in the scores which arises due to chance. If the chance variation is likely to have produced the difference between our groups, we say the difference is non-significant, which means the difference probably did arise from chance variation. We have to conclude there is no 'real' or statistically significant difference between the groups, and they are both from the same underlying population.

B6.2 Significance level

If the difference between two groups is likely to have arisen from chance variation in the scores, we conclude there is no real 'significant' difference between them. On the other hand, if the difference between the groups is unlikely to have been brought about by the chance variation in scores, we conclude there is a real, statistically significant difference between the groups.

But what do we mean by likely? It is conventional to use the 5% probability level (also referred to as alpha-level): what does this mean? If there is a 5% (also written as 0.05) or smaller probability that the difference between the groups arose from chance variation, we conclude it did not arise from chance and that there is a 'real' difference. If there is more than 5% (0.05) probability that the difference arose from chance, we conclude the difference is not a real one.

You may well ask why we use 5%; and the answer is that it is merely convention. We could use 10% (.10), 1% (.01), .5% (.005).

B6.3 Type I and type II errors

A significance test allows us to say how likely it is that the difference between the groups of subjects' scores was due to chance. If there is a 5% or smaller probability that the difference is due to chance variation, we conclude that it was not caused by chance. But we can never be sure: there is always a possibility that the difference we find was due to chance even when we conclude that it was not. Conversely, we may find a difference and conclude that it is not significant (that it was due to random or chance variability in the scores) when in fact it was a 'real' difference. So there are two types of error we may make. These are referred to as type I and type II errors.

A Type I error occurs when we reject a null hypothesis when it is true i.e we say there is a 'real' difference between the groups when in fact the difference is not 'real'. The probability that we shall make a type I error is given by the significance level we use. With an alpha or significance level of 5%, on 5% of occasions we are likely to make a type I error and say the groups differ when they do not.

We can reduce the probability of making a type I error by using a more stringent level of significance: 1%, say, rather than 5%. But as we reduce the chances of making a type I error, we increase the likelihood that we shall make a type II error, and say there is no difference between the groups when there is one.

B6.4 One and two-tailed hypotheses

Referring back to Table B3, the aim of the study was to test the hypothesis that there is a difference between the scores of the two groups of subjects. (The null hypothesis is that there is no difference between the scores of the two groups of subjects.)

Note that the hypothesis is that there is a difference. It does NOT say group 3 will score higher or lower than group 2, merely that group 3 and group 2 will differ. This is a two-tailed hypothesis: group 3 could score less than group 2 or group 3 could score more than group 2.

If we had stated the hypothesis that group 2 will score less than group 3 (i.e if we predict the direction of the difference between the groups), then we would have had a one-tail hypothesis. Similarly, if our hypothesis were that group 2 would score more than group 3, this would also be a one-tailed hypothesis since we would still be predicting the direction of the difference between the groups.

The distinction between one and two-tailed hypotheses is important when applying significance tests. Most SPSS/PC+ printouts show the two-tailed probability of the calculated statistic. If you have stated a one-tailed hypothesis before examining the data, you can use the one-tailed probabilities, which are the two-tailed probabilities divided by 2.

B7 Parametric and non-parametric tests

Parametric significance tests rest upon assumptions that the data has certain characteristics. The assumptions for using parametric tests are:

1. Observations are drawn from a population with a normal distribution (note that the population is normally distributed, not necessarily the sample of scores taken from it)

2. The sets of data being compared have approximately equal variances (this is referred to as homogeneity of variance). If the groups are of equal size ($n_1 = n_2$), then this assumption is not so important as it is when the two groups have unequal n's. If the groups being compared have an n of 10, is is acceptable for the variance of one group to be up to three times as large as that of another. With larger groups, you can still use the parametric tests if one group has a variance double that of another.

3. The data is measured on an interval scale.

If the data does not meet these assumptions, you can convert the data into a non-parametric form and then apply one of the non-parametric tests. The commonest way of converting data into a form for non-parametric analysis is to rank it.

B8 Analyzing nominal data: Chi-square

B8.1 The two-way chi-square

The chi-square test is used with nominal (frequency) data, where subjects are assigned to categories. For example, a recent survey asked adults whether they thought 'adult' films should be shown uncut on TV. Data was reported for different age groups and sexes.

The results for men might have looked like this:

Table B4. Male respondents' views on showing uncut films on TV
(hypothetical data).

Respondents' age	Number saying 'yes'	Number saying 'no'
under 60	75	35
over 60	50	30

The cell entries show the number of respondents of that age-group giving the response indicated at the top of the column.

The chi-square test is used for analyzing this type of frequency data, and is concerned with answering the question: Is there a relationship between the variable that distinguishes the rows (age, in the example above) and the variable that distinguishes the columns (response 'yes' or 'no' in the example)?

The test rests upon comparing the observed frequencies with the 'expected' frequencies which would be obtained if there were no relationship between the row variable and the column variable. (The expected frequencies are calculated for each cell in the table by multiplying the appropriate row and column totals and dividing by N.)

An example of the SPSS/PC+ output from a chi-square test is shown in Fig 14.2. It states the probability of the value of chi-square having arisen by chance.

B8.2 The one-sample chi-square

The test can be used with just one sample of data. In section 18.3, the example of suicide rates for different months is used to explain the way one would employ the one-sample chi-square. The result of applying a one-sample chi-square is shown in Fig 18.1.

B8.3 Essential requirements for the chi-square test

The chi-square test is only valid if three conditions are met. First, the data must be independent: no subject can appear in more than one cell of the table. In Table B4, this condition is met since any person is either under or over 60 and any person responded yes or no.

Secondly, no more than 20% of the Expected Frequencies in the table can be less than 5. So if you have a 2 x 5 table which has 10 cells, the test will be invalid if 3 expected frequencies are below 5. If your data fails to meet this criterion, you have to collect more data or it may be possible to change the table; for example you could merge groups together. SPSS/PC+ output from the two-way chi-square test (Fig 14.3) indicates the number of cells with an expected frequency of less than 5, and shows the number of cells as a percentage, so you can readily see if the data meets this criterion or not.

Thirdly, no cell should have an expected frequency of less than 1. The printed output (Fig 14.3) tells you the minimum expected frequency so it is simple to check whether this condition has been met.

B9 Parametric tests

B9.1 The t-test

The t-test is a parametric test which is used to test whether the difference between the means of two sets of scores is statistically significant.

There is one important feature of the t-test. If you have more than two sets of data, it is not acceptable to do multiple t-tests. For example, assume we have measured the performance of three groups of subjects (groups A, B and C) on a test of memory. It is not valid to do one t-test to compare groups A and B, another to compare B and C and another to compare A and C. The reason is that multiple t-testing distorts the probability levels: when you believe you are using the 5% level, you are not. If you have data from three groups, you should use a test designed to cope with that situation. For parametric data, this is the analysis of variance. For non-parametric data you can use Friedman's test (repeated measures) or the Kruskal-Wallis test (independent groups).

You need to be sure about when it is appropriate to use the independent t-test and when to use the related test. (Essentially, if you use a related t-test when you should have used an independent one, you may conclude that the difference is significant when it is not- a type I error).

B9.1.1 The independent t-test

The independent t-test is used to compare the means of two groups of subjects i.e when different individuals were allocated to group 1 and group 2. It involves taking the difference between the means, and expressing that difference as a ratio of the variability of the scores in the two sets.

The output from having SPSS/PC+ perform a between-subjects t-test is shown in Fig 16.3. It gives the value of t, the degrees of freedom and the two-tailed probability.

B9.1.2 The related, paired or within-subjects t-test

Use the related t-test when comparing the means of two sets of scores obtained with the same subjects in both conditions. This form of t-test involves calculating the difference between the two scores for each respondent, finding the mean of these differences and expressing it as a ratio of the variability of the difference scores. An example is given in section 16.3, with the output shown in Fig 16.2.

B9.2 Analysis of Variance

B9.2.1 Basic concepts

When you have three or more sets of parametric data, you may want to test the hypothesis that the scores of the various groups differ. You cannot use the t-test, as that only compares two groups and it is not proper to carry out multiple t-tests on three sets of data. The parametric analysis of variance is the technique to employ; it makes the same assumptions as the t-test, so should only be used when those assumptions (see section B7 above) can be made.

As the name implies analysis of variance examines the variance within the whole sets of scores. Imagine we have sets of data from three separate groups of subjects, and want to know whether there is a difference between the three groups. If there were no difference between the groups (the null hypothesis is true) their data would all come from the same population, and the three sets of data would all have the same means and the same variances. The variance of each group would be an estimate of the population variance (variance due to random fluctuations between subjects, known as error variance because it arises due to chance alterations in our readings). Our best estimate of the population variance is given by calculating the mean of the variances of the three groups. So by looking at the average variance of the three groups, we can get an estimate of the error variance.

Again, if the null hypothesis is true, the means of the three groups will be the same, and the variance of the means (i.e how much the means differ from each other) will be very small. (We would expect it to be the same as the population variance.) The variance of the means of the three groups is known as the treatment variance. So if the null hypothesis were true, and the three groups did not differ from each other, the variance between the means (the treatment variance) would equal the error variance; if we divided the treatment variance by the error variance, the answer would be 1.00.

If the null hypothesis is not true, there is a difference between the three groups. The variance of the means will be larger than the error variance. If we divide the variance of the means (the treatment variance) by the error variance, we shall get a number bigger than 1.00.

In the analysis of variance, we compare the treatment variance with the error variance
to test the hypothesis that there is a significant difference between the means.

B9.2.2 Obtaining one-way anovar

The one-way anovar is obtained using either MEANS or ONEWAY, described in
section 16.2. The output from ONEWAY is illustrated in Fig 16.1. The crucial
statistic is the value of F, the ratio of the mean square due to treatments (between
groups) and the mean square due to error (within groups). The output shows the
probability of the calculated value of F arising by chance; if this value is less than
0.05 one can conclude there is a significant difference between the groups.

B9.2.3 Two-way anovar

Analysis of variance can be extended to experiments in which there are two or more
independent variables. Imagine we have measured the performance of young (under
30) and old (over 50) subjects at two different times of day (2 am and 2 pm), and
used different subjects in each group so there were four separate groups altogether.
We might be interested in knowing whether performance differed according to the
subject's age, differed according to time of day, and whether there was an interaction
between these variables. Interaction means that the effect of one variable was
influenced by the other; for example, we might find that the difference between
performance at 2 pm and 2 am was less for the younger subjects than for the older
ones. If this were so, the analysis of variance would show a significant interaction
term.

When both variables are between-subjects, as in the example just given, the ANOVA
procedure is used. An example of its output is provided in Fig 16.4.

The analysis of variance can be applied to within-subjects (repeated measures)
studies, where the same subjects are used in diffferent conditions. For example, we
would have a repeated measures experiment if we had carried out our time-of-day /
age of subjects experiment, and tested the same respondents at 2 am and 2 pm. To
analyse this kind of experiment requires the MANOVA procedure not covered here as
it is not part of the base module of SPSS/PC+ Version 3. An explanation of
MANOVA is provided in the manual for the Advanced Statistics module.

B9.2.4 Range tests

If the analysis of variance indicates a significant F value, you can conclude there is a
difference between the three or more groups that were compared. But the anovar does
not indicate which groups differed from which: was group A different from both B
and C, or were A and B very similar but both different from group C? To answer
these questions, one needs to use multiple comparison procedures. A number of these
are available, including the Tukey test, the Scheffe test, the Duncan test. The relative
merits of these tests is too advanced to be considered here, but the Tukey HSD

(Honestly Significant Differences) test is widely used. The multiple comparison tests are obtained using the ONEWAY procedure (section 16.2 and Fig 16.1).

B10 Correlation

B10.1 The concept of correlation

A correlation expresses the extent to which two variables vary together. A positive correlation means that as one variable increases so does the other. For example, there is a strong positive correlation between size of foot and height, and a weak positive correlation between how much one is paid and one's job satisfaction. A negative correlation is when one variable increases as the other decreases; for example, there is a negative correlation between job satisfaction and absenteeism: the more satisfied people are with their job, the lower the amount of absenteeism they show.

Correlations vary between –1.00 and +1.00; a correlation of 0.00 means there is no relationship between the two variables. For example, one would expect the correlation between size of foot and job satisfaction to be about 0.00 (although I have never seen any data on this relationship!)

There is one vital factor about correlations, summarized in the aphorism "Correlation does not equal causation": if variables A and B are correlated, one cannot say that A causes B. It could be that B causes A, or they may both be related to some other factor that produces the variation in A and B. Some examples: absenteeism and job satisfaction are negatively correlated, but one cannot conclude that low job satisfaction causes absenteeism; it is possible that being absent a lot causes the feelings of low job satisfaction. The positive correlation between foot size and height does not mean that having a large foot makes you grow; foot size and overall height are both caused by a common genetic factor.

However, correlations are used to predict one variable from another. Knowing someone's foot size, one can predict how tall they are better than one could if you did not know their foot size.

B10.2 Parametric correlation: Pearson product moment correlation

This is the parametric measure of correlation, and measures the relationship between two variables which have both been measured on an interval scale. It is obtained with the CORRELATIONS procedure (section 17.1). The output is illustrated in Fig 17.1, and shows the significance of r by asterisks.

B10.3 Non-parametric correlation: Spearman Rank (rho)

This is a non-parametric correlation and can be used when data is ordinal rather than interval.

To obtain rho, the data for each measure must be on a rank scale and the CORRELATIONS procedure used, as explained in section 18.9.

B10.4 Regression

When two variables are correlated, one can predict the level of an individual on variable x from their standing on variable y (or vice versa: one can predict height from foot size or one can predict foot size from height). When you have a scattergram (Fig 17.2), it is possible to draw in the best-fitting straight line that represents the relationship between x and y by connecting the R printed on the left vertical axis with the R on the right vertical axis. The PLOT /FORMAT REGRESSION procedure described in section 17.2 gives the slope of the line (how steeply it rises) and the intercept (the point at which it meets the horizontal axis of the graph). The best-fitting line is known as the regression line and it can be expressed as an equation of the form x = c + by, where c is the intercept and b the slope.

The correlation coefficient squared (r^2) indicates how much of the variance in y is explained by x. So if x correlates with y 0.6, then .36 (36%) of the variance in y is explained by the variance in x.

B10.5 Multiple regression

This refers to using more than one variable to predict the dependent variable. Job satisfaction is correlated with pay and with level of occupation. So one can predict job satisfaction from pay and one can predict it from job satisfaction; but one may get a better prediction if one uses both pay and job level as predictors. So one would have an equation of the form:

job satisfaction = pay multiplied by a + level of job multiplied by b

This is an example of a multiple regression equation, where the dependent variable is related to a number of independent, or predictor, variables. Each predictor variable is multiplied by a weighting, reflecting its importance in determining the dependent, or predicted, variable. The weighting is known as the regression coefficient for that variable.

In multiple regression analysis, one investigates which variables add to one's ability to predict the dependent variable, and the weighting they should have. So one has a file of data including the dependent variable and the predictor variable scores for each respondent. The REGRESSION procedure (section 17.3) is used to find out which predictors add to one's ability to predict the dependent variable and what their regression coefficients are.

There are a number of alternative techniques that one can use in solving a multiple regression problem, using the /METHOD subcommand of REGRESSION. For example, one can force all the predictor variables to be included in the equation, or one can have the program calculate the predictive power of each one and only include those which add to the accuracy with which the dependent variable is predicted. The SPSS/PC+ Manual provides full details on the various methods.

B11 Nonparametric tests

B11.1 Deciding which test to use

When the assumptions underlying parametric tests are not met, non-parametric tests can be applied. The chi-square test (section 8 above) deals with nominal (frequency) data. The four non-parametric tests described in this section are used to analyze the subjects' dependent variable measures.

To decide which test to apply you can follow this decision tree:

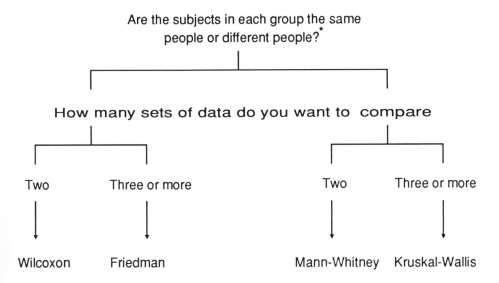

* If you have formed *matched groups* of subjects, you can assume you have the 'same' people in the groups i.e it is a within-Ss experiment.

B11.2 Wilcoxon test

If you have carried out a within-subjects experiment, and have two scores for each subject, the Wilcoxon test is used to see whether there is a significant difference between the subjects' scores under the two conditions.

It involves calculating the differences between the scores for each subject, and ranking the difference scores, giving rank 1 to the smallest difference etc, but ignoring the sign of the difference. Any subjects where the difference score is 0 are dropped from the analysis. The + or − signs of the difference scores are assigned to the rank values, and the sum of the rank-values obtained for the + and − signed ranks separately.

The Wilcoxon test rests on the argument that if there is no difference between the two sets of scores, there will be about the same number of small + differences as there are small − differences, and about the same number of large + differences as there are large − differences. So the sum of the ranks for + differences will be about the same as the sum of the ranks for the − differences. If the sums of + differences are very dissimilar to the sum of the − differences, then it is likely there is a reliable difference between the two sets of scores.

An example of the output from a Wilcoxon test is given in Fig 18.2. It gives a value of z and the associated probability.

B11.3 Friedman test

This is used to compare three or more groups of matched subjects. A table is created where each row is the data for one subject, and the data within each row is ranked. The sum of ranks (T) for each column is calculated.

Friedman's test is concerned with establishing whether the rank totals of each column differ more than would be expected by chance; if there were no difference between the conditions, the rank totals would be more or less the same. The output from this test is given in Fig 18.3, and provides a value for chi-square and its significance.

B11.4 Mann-Whitney

This is used to compare two sets of data obtained from independent groups. The whole collection of scores are ranked, the sum of the rank values of each subgroup is calculated, and a U statistic is then calculated. The value of U is transformed into a z-value in the output for this test (Fig 18.4).

B11.5 Kruskal-Wallis

This test is used with three or more independent groups (between subjects design). The method is reminiscent of the Mann-Whitney, in that it involves ranking all the scores and then calculating the sum of ranks for each group. The output (Fig 18.5) gives a value of chi-square and its probability.

B12 Interpreting the outcome of a significance test

Understanding what a significance test tells you is the most important part of statistical analysis: doing all the proper tests and getting the correct answers is no good if you then misunderstand what the outcome means! Unfortunately, in the drive to do the computations, some investigators forget that the interpretation is the rationale for the whole procedure. So try to remember some basic principles:

1. If the test tells you the difference between groups is not significant, you must conclude there is no difference, even though the mean scores are not identical

2. If the difference between groups is statistically significant, this does NOT necessarily mean that it is practically meaningful or significant in the everyday sense. For example, in a study of people's ability to remember car licence plates, one group's score remained the same on two test occasions so the increase was 0, whereas another group's score increased from 3.22 to 3.42, an increase of 0.20; the difference was statistically significant. But it is a subjective judgement, not a statistical one, as to whether the increase of 0.20 for the second group has any practical importance.

3. The assumption behind the experimental method is that one can conclude that significant changes in the dependent variable are caused by the changes in the independent variable. But the validity of this assumption depends on one having used a properly designed and controlled experiment: just because one has a significant difference between group A and group B doe NOT mean you can necessarily conclude the difference was due to the changes in the independent variable. If the experiment was confounded, and the different groups differed systematically on another variable in addition to the independent variable, no clear explanation of the differences in the dependent variable can be given. Imagine we compare two schemes for teaching reading: group A has one scheme and group B the other. We find that group B learn to read after a shorter period of instruction. Can we conclude that the scheme used by group B is 'better'? We now discover that all the children in group B are from a higher socio-economic group than the children in group A (i.e the experiment was confounded). This means that differences between the group's reading may have been due to home background, not the reading scheme they were given. So the statistical significance of the result does not by itself give us any

grounds for concluding that the independent variable brought about the changes in the dependent variable.

4. Avoid the temptation to take the level of significance as an index of the magnitude of the experimental effect. By convention one usually uses the 5% significance level, but one can use a more stringent one, and find that a difference between groups is significant not only at 5% but also at 1% or 0.1%. Even eminent researchers have been known to argue that a difference significant at 1% is somehow more 'real' than one significant at 5%. This is NOT a valid interpretation. If the result of your analysis is significant at the level you are using (usually 5%), just accept that and do not give in to the temptation to conclude that a difference significant at 1% is 'better'!

INDEX